Rainbows
After
the STORM

Rainbows After the STORM

An Empowering Approach to Overcoming the Trials of Life

DIANE SANTOS

Copyright © 2017 Diane Santos
Rainbows After the Storm
All rights reserved.
Published by Cardinal Rules Press
Cover Design by Diane Santos
Formatted by Diane Santos
Edited by Marley Gibson
ISBN-13: 978-1546802891
ISBN-10: 1546802894

This story is based on the personal experiences of the author. In some instances names have been changed in the interest of protecting personal privacy. No part of this book shall be reproduced or transmitted in any form or by any means, electronic, mechanical, magnetic, photographic including photocopying, recording or by any information storage and retrieval system, without prior written permission of the author, except in the case of brief quotations embodied in critical articles and reviews. No patent liability is assumed with respect to the use of the information contained herein. Although every precaution has been taken in the preparation of this book, the publisher and author assume no responsibility for errors or omissions. Neither is any liability assumed for damages resulting from the use of the information contained herein.

Any Internet references contained in the work are current at publication time, but cannot guarantee that a specific location will continue to be maintained.

DEDICATION

For Mom and Dad, with appreciation…

*Your countless sacrifices and shining example
helped mold me into the woman I am today*

Mary Clara (Rozario) Santos
October 14, 1932 – June 10, 1996

Abel Manuel Santos
April 29, 1930 – January 11, 2005

~~ Always Missed and Forever Loved ~~

TABLE OF CONTENTS

ACKNOWLEDGEMENTS i
Chapter One – Growing Through the Pain 1
Chapter Two – Necessary Forgiveness 10
Chapter Three – Leap of Faith 20
Chapter Four – Heart to Heart 27
Chapter Five – A Purpose Revealed 36
Chapter Six – No Distance Between Souls 51
Chapter Seven – Encouraging Occurrences 58
Chapter Eight – Forward Motion 66
Chapter Nine – Unshakable Foundation 73
Chapter Ten – An Open Book 82
Chapter Eleven – Tangible Reminders 92
Chapter Twelve – The Fact of the Matter 103
Chapter Thirteen – Whispers From Within 114
Chapter Fourteen – Intentional Diversion 127
Chapter Fifteen – New Considerations 135
Chapter Sixteen – Visual Effects 142
Chapter Seventeen – Spreading the Wealth 149
Chapter Eighteen – The Human Factor 157
Chapter Nineteen – Kindred Spirits 166
Chapter Twenty – All in the Approach 174
Chapter Twenty-One – The Road Ahead 187
EPILOGUE 194
RECIPE FOR A JOYFUL LIFE 199
PHOTOS 202
ABOUT THE AUTHOR 208

ACKNOWLEDGEMENTS

My eternal gratitude to Michael Tyrone Johnson, "Tyger" for remaining with me always. Souls do not recognize this temporary separation known as death. You entered my world as a breath of fresh air. Everything changed for the better in our physical time together. Thank you for guiding me in all I do. You are now, and will forever be, my greatest source of inspiration.

Aaron Michael, you give me countless reasons to smile. You were born with the spirit of a warrior, proving every doctor wrong when they said my baby wouldn't make it. The fighter within is helping you realize the strength and courage you possess. Your independent nature drives you to keep pushing. I love you son, and I'm proud of the man you are.

Mark Andrew, from a young age you filled our lives with laughter. I cherish the many "Markie stories" going back to your childhood. You've grown into a responsible adult with a caring, generous heart. Your admirable qualities of self-confidence and humility are a source of pride and joy, my son. Thank you for always assuring me, "all will be well." I love you.

My dearest Sophia Lynn, my heart overflows with love for you. I can't imagine life without your beautiful presence. You express compassion for others and view the world through selfless eyes. Nani was blessed the day you were born. Mike watches over you. Keep listening for his messages with an open heart.

A relative who speaks the same spiritual language is a source of comfort. That's what I have in you, Crystal Marie. Our level of understanding makes it possible to discuss any topic without the need of watering it down. Grateful to your Mom for choosing me as your Godmother. You hold a special place in my heart and I love you beyond the moon and stars.

Family and friends, your ongoing support assures me I never walk alone. I would love nothing more than to mention you all by name, but the list would be endless. That fact is a testament to how blessed I am to be surrounded by such a nurturing village of people. Thank you for accompanying me on this journey, through both rough and calm seas. I love you all.

It is such a pleasure working with you, Marley Gibson. You are an exceptional editor, best-selling author, talented chef, and so much more. I honestly don't know when you sleep. My thanks for your diligence in ensuring my work is polished and well-presented. You are simply amazing.

To my spiritual angels, Laura and Lee, you are greatly appreciated. The warmth of your beautiful light emanates peace and love. Each of you continues to play a significant role in the progression of my enlightenment. Thank you for sharing your gifts with me.

As I align with the wonders of the Universe, my connection to a higher consciousness is strengthened. Source energy, God, the eternal light, flows through me. This same current, tapped into by the great spiritual leaders of past and present, is available to all. We are love in its purest, most unadulterated form, and for this, I am grateful.

Chapter One
Growing Through the Pain

WHERE DOES ONE TURN when life blindsides you with a crushing blow?

This is what I asked myself following the sudden passing of the man I loved.

Michael Tyrone Johnson was affectionately known by some as "Big Mike," in reference to his size. He was a towering six-foot, five inches tall and a solid four hundred pounds. His massive frame could be a formidable sight, but housed a compassionate, caring soul.

Family members called him "Tyger" for as far back as anyone could remember, as did friends in the town where we'd both grown up. Tyger had been my entire world and in one split second, he was gone. His time was cut short unexpectedly due to heart failure. The pain I experienced was unlike anything I'd ever known and it left me wanting to die.

Every minute was spent pleading with God to end my suffering by taking me, also. There seemed to be no reason to go on when each new day found me just as miserable as the one before.

There is no preparing for the devastation of having your happiness ripped away without warning. The heartache is felt in every way imaginable... physically, mentally, emotionally, and spiritually. Each waking moment is filled with reminders of what's been lost.

Imagine falling asleep peacefully in your bed only to awaken the next morning in a foreign country. Nothing about this strange land is familiar and not a single soul speaks your language. If you can envision how you'd feel, it will give you a tiny glimpse of what I was going through in the days, weeks, and months following Tyger's death. I was isolated, alone, and utterly lost.

However, a miraculous transformation took place as Tyger began sending messages from the other side. To me, this was undeniable proof that he was still very much alive and always close. Receiving signs from Tyger provided hope, yet I doubted my own judgment. Was my mind playing tricks on me as some sort of coping mechanism for my agony?

The answer came when I made the decision to meet with a spiritual medium. My desire to get back into life was sparked by what took place during that reading. As I sat listening to this woman, a virtual stranger to me, I was captivated by what she shared; her ability to relay Tyger's thoughts exactly as he would have. My heart absolutely knew Tyger was right there and those were *his* words she was speaking. That was the day I became a true believer in the existence of life beyond physical death.

One hour. That's the length of time it took to prove to me I had some serious rethinking to do. I went into our meeting open-minded and cautiously optimistic. Little did I know those sixty minutes would become a pivotal event in my life. Reflecting on it now, I can say with absolute certainty it turned out to be just that. A metamorphosis began to take place deep within; an awakening to new truths. Suddenly, it was evident the vast majority of what I had been taught to believe didn't quite add up. Not only was I coming to terms with how expansive life actually is, I had to develop an entirely new line of reasoning. This meant a complete stripping away of the limiting thought processes imposed on me by religion and society, in general.

I poured my heart and soul into my first book, *Onward Into the Light: A True Story of Profound Love, Devastating Loss, and a Bond Unbroken by Death*. My personal views on what happens when we die were also shared, with complete awareness of the repercussions that may result. Well-meaning friends have suggested the disclosure of my beliefs on what lies beyond the physical could create a backlash. They warn that these views may be perceived as going against the teachings of certain faiths, so I should tread lightly. I've been cautioned on the possibility of offending or alienating those who disagree. It's a chance I am more than willing to take, though, because the message is so important. The potential to offer hope and validate experiences far outweighs any fallout from those who might disagree. To put it plainly, if anyone were to feel put-off by what I discuss in my writings, then it obviously isn't for them.

Our story continues to make its way to family and friends and I am pleasantly surprised by their reactions. For some, it seems to give them the freedom to discuss occurrences in their own lives. There are those who choose to tell me—privately—how much they can relate to my thoughts and feelings. Others are very open and publicly voice their agreement with the subject matter. Regardless of the method of delivery, I'm assured by their comments that the topic is powerful and impacting many lives.

Casual conversations often lead to unexpected tales of contact from the other side. At a routine dental visit, I told the hygienist, a woman named Catherine, that I'd written a book. She asked what it was about and I explained it was a telling of my grief journey since losing the love of my life. She congratulated me and said how wonderful it was that I was willing to help others who've lost someone. I wasn't prepared to hear what followed, but I sat glued to her every word.

"Have you received messages from him since his death?"

Her question was music to my ears, as it indicated she was a believer.

"Oh yes," I answered right away. "He communicates all the time in many different ways. I go into great detail in the book."

My response assured her it was safe to continue. "I believe my mother communicates with me," Catherine said. She officially had my undivided attention and my expression encouraged her to go on.

"As a child, my mom explained to me how she'd chosen my name. She was an avid reader and during her pregnancy, she read 'Catherine of Siena' written by a Norwegian author in the early 1900s. When I was born, she decided I would be Catherine, after the main character in this old book. Several years after my mom passed, a female patient came in carrying a book. I glanced at the cover and it was the same one my mother had spoken of. I was curious so I asked how she'd come to read this particular story. The woman told me her husband had found it lying on the side of the road, so he picked it up and brought it home. She decided to bring it along to read in the waiting room before her appointment."

I reacted to this experience with astonishment. It was such an obvious sign from Catherine's mother and I relayed my thoughts on what she'd shared. "That was your mother's doing, her way of connecting with you."

The look on her face was one of relief as she said, "I took it as my mom telling me she is okay."

I smiled as I replied assuredly, "Believe what your heart is telling you. The odds of a rare book with such importance to you, making its way into your company, are a million to one. Not to mention the unorthodox way it was found, lying outside as though someone had left it there."

She was grateful for my reassurance and said she'd wondered if she was reading too much into it. I showed her the goose bumps on my arms, a physical reaction to her powerful connection with her mother and said, "Don't you doubt it for a minute. Our loved ones are always close."

This is one of many accounts I've had the pleasure of hearing about. In some cases, these individuals have never mentioned the intimate details of their ongoing connections to another living soul. Each time, I express my appreciation for their trust in relaying something so sacred to them. The effects of these associations are mutually beneficial. On their part, it's the comfort of having someone to confide in without fear of judgment. For me, it's continued solid affirmations of the authenticity of these communications.

Incidents such as Catherine's confirm the importance of telling others about the connection Tyger and I maintain between worlds. Catherine probably had few people she was comfortable enough with to disclose this beautiful message from her deceased mother. Although she and I share no personal history, she recognized the safety of opening up on a subject some consider taboo.

My drive to move forward is powered by these types of interactions. I have the honor of providing a platform where the bereaved can find validation and understanding. There is such peace in knowing others are finding solace and a place of refuge by reading my words. Discovering one is not alone has incredible healing properties. My intent is to continue facilitating a safe-haven for those facing any form of tragedy.

In my personal opinion, the existence of an afterlife is accepted by far more than are willing to admit. Their hesitation is a result of not wanting to be labeled as "crazy" or "weird." Not everyone is prepared to be as vocal about their beliefs as I am which is completely understandable. There was a time in my life when, like them, I chose to remain silent. My concern was the opinions of others if I strayed too far from what the majority had deemed reasonable.

I have reached the point where I require approval from no one other than my higher self. If some relationships become strained by my views, it simply means we're on different courses. I believe we all have pieces of the whole truth. Our paths to getting there aren't laid out like a grid of city blocks. They are filled with unpredictable twists and turns. We may travel in the same direction for part of the way, then take a turn and arrive at new conclusions. The point is to keep going and growing.

I'm fond of the Hindu Proverb, "There are hundreds of paths up the mountain, all leading to the same place, so it doesn't matter which path you take. The only person wasting time is the one who runs around the mountain, telling everyone his or her path is wrong."

Readers ranging from non-religious to devout Christians and everything in between have confided in me about encounters with what some would call the supernatural. For those who don't accept the possibility of remaining connected between realms, it's the love in our story which resonates with them. There is no need for me to shy away from speaking my truth. Even those who don't fully agree have witnessed the positive impact on my overall outlook and the resurgence of a will to continue.

Connecting with Tyger since his transition has given me permission to go on living. My desire to push forward began there, but the momentum is fueled by my ever-grateful heart. Even at my lowest point, I remained thankful for the positive effect of our love and all we shared in our physical time together.

Now that I've emerged from the darkness, my dominant emotion is gratitude. I find joy in expressing appreciation for what I have and the beautiful memories we made. Focusing on the enhancement of my life experience, rather than what was lost, has literally made the difference between begging to die and choosing to live.

I'm amazed by the evolution taking place as I continue adjusting to life without Tyger's physical presence. I went from the euphoric state of being completely loved to the darkest depths of grief and despair, to then slowly seeing the light of a new day again. During the process, I discovered the undeniable: there is no end to us. With that came the realization of how wasteful it is to spend our time in fear. The same applies to worry, which is another exercise in futility. I realize how often I've held myself back from trying new things because of my own fear. Those feelings have been eliminated from my world and, for the first time ever, my mind is free.

The majority of my life, thus far, has been spent as a quiet introvert. While my basic demeanor hasn't changed much, I am now capable of verbalizing my opinions. Tyger continues to drive and inspire me toward my purpose. I credit him with many of the ideas that come to me, seemingly out of nowhere. My reaction is to write those thoughts down, even if they don't immediately make sense. I am always mindful of a message, delivered a year or so after his passing by an intuitive friend. Tyger stated we have something very important to do together. My interpretation of his words is that our story must continue to be told. We are obligated to share this truth with others, not only as a source of hope, but as part of an overall awakening. A remembering of who we really are and why we're here.

Symbolically, I consider myself as having been through the fire of discovery. Those old belief systems were consumed by the flames along with any anxiety or self-doubt. This purging has birthed a new, improved version of Diane. Some original traits remain, but I'm now equipped to handle the responsibilities that lie before me. I have risen from the ashes as my true, authentic self, willing to share my journey in order to light the way for others.

Even as I miss Tyger's physical presence, his passing sparked my new state of being. I feel his happiness as I embrace this positive outlook. Each morning holds the promise of wonder and excitement; like a blank page waiting to be written. My soul eagerly anticipates what lies ahead.

As the author of my future, I'll accept no less than a thrilling ride. After all, today is the first day of the rest of my life…

Chapter Two
Necessary Forgiveness

MY TRAVELS SINCE TYGER'S TRANSITION have led me to some unexpected places.

As I clawed my way out of the darkness, I was forced to reassess everything. Not only did I discover most of my beliefs lacked authenticity, the woman staring back at me in the mirror was different, as well.

Prior to my relationship with Tyger, I'd spent the majority of my life with low self-esteem. I'm not sure how this came about, but it surfaced during my teen years; an overall sense of not being good enough. This inferiority complex had some roots in my appearance. The usual culprits of acne and fluctuations in weight were definite factors. My facial features seemed to draw compliments, so I was aware of being attractive, but not in a conceited way. Getting good grades came naturally and I had no problem making friends. I was far from an outcast, yet I never quite fit in.

My bashful persona made communicating difficult, so I was usually quiet. In most cases, my silence was a combination of not knowing what to say and the uncontrollable redness that appeared in my cheeks anytime all eyes were on me. To avoid sounding ridiculous and the unnecessary blushing, I kept my words to myself. This was interpreted by some as being "stuck up" which was not the case at all. Since I didn't readily join the crowd, there were girls who chose to dislike me. They assumed I thought I was better than them. If they only knew how wrong they were.

I grew up in Norwich, Connecticut, on a side of town which was predominately white. Although I am very fair-skinned, my race is not Caucasian or Latino, as many assume when they see me. Both my maternal and paternal grandparents came from Cape Verde, an archipelago of volcanic islands, approximately 350 miles off the west coast of Africa, near Senegal.

The islands were ruled for many years by Portugal; used primarily as a penal colony during the height of the slave trade. The culture is a blend of African and Portuguese customs, as is the language known as "Kriolu." There is a vast difference in skin tones and hair textures among the Cape Verdean, stemming from the heavy European influence.

Mankind has developed a preoccupation with assigning labels when it pertains to one's ethnicity. Given my background, I suppose I'd be classified as African American or American with Afro/Euro roots. Either would be accurate and I can identify with both. However, I consider myself an American woman of Cape Verdean descent, who takes great pride in her heritage. Anyone who cares to sort out the lineage is more than welcome to have at it. At the end of the day, I'm a member of the human race, so that should be all that matters.

Cape Verdeans are proud, hard-working people who are highly family-oriented. Both my parents come from large families; my mother was the fourth of twelve children and my father was the fifth of ten. Although born in the U. S., neither of them learned English until they began attending school because it wasn't spoken in the home.

During the 1800s, Cape Verdeans began migrating to the United States, mainly aboard whaling ships. The majority settled in the port towns of New England; New Bedford, Massachusetts and Providence, Rhode Island being the most common, then radiating outward from there toward Boston and into Connecticut.

In the years since, Cape Verdeans have settled across the United States and Europe. There is a high population in the Scandinavian countries, as well. My maternal grandfather arrived in this country aboard the whaling schooner *Valkyria* in the 1920s. His name, Antonio Manuel Rozario, can be found listed in the ship's manifest at the New Bedford Whaling Museum.

As the immigrants arrived on American shores, they learned quickly that it was in their best interest to deny the African connection and identify more closely with their European roots. The extreme prejudice against and atrocities being inflicted upon blacks was rampant, so it seemed the best chance for acceptance was to call themselves "Portuguese" which came with a white connotation. This decision was based on survival, but for some evolved into a complete denial of African bloodlines.

In some communities, Cape Verdeans considered it bad practice for their children to associate or mix with blacks.

As you can imagine, this had the potential to create an atmosphere of racial tension and it did in some areas. This was the case in my hometown, which has a fairly large Cape Verdean population. Thankfully, my parents were open-minded and never discouraged me from any friendships, regardless of race. Unfortunately, there were plenty of other families who weren't as enlightened.

This placed Cape Verdean youth in a no-man's-land, of sorts. Although we identified closely with the black culture in our choice of music and fashion, we weren't readily accepted. On the other hand, since many of us were brown-skinned, the white community didn't embrace us either.

Believe it or not, even in the midst of so much controversy, I never gave much thought to skin color during my childhood. In elementary school, most of the students were white. Although I knew I wasn't, it was no cause for concern. We played together and many bonds were formed.

Imagine my surprise when it came time to move on to junior high and I introduced my classmate to a cousin with a dark complexion. I'll never forget the girl's facial expression when she turned to me and asked, "You're *black*?"

My response was, "You thought I was white?"

Neither of us meant anything malicious by our remarks. We were equally caught off guard.

This ethnic divide became more pronounced in high school. In many cases, an overall discord existed between Cape

Verdean girls and other female members of the black community. There was a perception we considered ourselves superior with our light skin and straight hair. I can't speak for everyone, but in my case, that simply wasn't true. Personally, I embrace my African heritage; however, there is no denying the European influence. It's apparent each time I look in the mirror.

The air of conflict coupled with this burden of avoiding attention at all costs became a recipe for disaster in someone already suffering from low self-esteem. Regardless of their reasons, the fact that some disliked me only fueled my conviction of being "less than."

This sub-standard mindset carried over into my romantic experiences and I fell into a pattern of accepting the treatment of others. Rather than demand respect, I settled for what the other person was willing to give. I didn't realize it at the time, but this was laying the groundwork for some terrible disappointments in my future.

Along with two unsuccessful marriages, I've had more than one semi-long-term relationship that, for some reason or another, didn't work out. My heart has been subjected to quite a bit over the years, yet it still has the capacity for love. It has survived being lied to, disrespected, betrayed, deceived, broken, and shattered into pieces. Of course, I played a role in the breakups, as well, so my intent is not to lay the blame solely on anyone else.

As difficult as it is to admit, I have been the victim in some abusive situations. Physical violence is damaging on so many levels because the emotional scars last long after the cuts and bruises have healed. For someone who was struggling with a diminished sense of value, these assaults felt deserved. On some level, I reasoned if only I'd been better, his treatment would have improved. Of course, I'm fully aware now of how flawed my logic was. The problem wasn't mine, but his. At the time, however, my thought process was nothing like it is today.

Rather than pack up and leave, I stayed, as many battered women do. The apologies seemed sincere as did the promises that "it would never happen again." Unfortunately, the incident wasn't isolated and I finally found the courage to gather my belongings and go. Any apprehension about starting over soon dissipated once the threat of physical harm was removed.

I was quite young when this abuse took place and eventually learned to trust again. The relationships that followed were better and I learned there *are* good men out there who don't resort to using their fists in order make a point.

My saving grace came when Tyger entered my life and improved every aspect of my existence. His all-encompassing love elevated me to a place of knowing how deserving I am of happiness. The admiration in his eyes convinced me I am worthy of respect and honesty. Our time together mended the breaks in my heart from the past and filled me with hope for the future.

In the course of our union, I never once considered what life would be like without him. His death forced me to decide if I would build on the foundation of confidence he filled me with or slide back into the insecure person I'd been before. As I emerged from my fragile state, I made a conscious decision to not only remain the woman he loved, but to continue growing, improving and expanding. As certain as I was, of course, I had to figure out how to get there.

It became evident the first step had to be forgiveness. I needed to purge myself of the deep injuries that plagued my history in order to move forward. Guilt and blame cause us to remain stuck in one place; restricted from the fullness of life. In order for me to progress, I first needed to go back and let go of any remaining negative emotions from my past.

As a mother, there is much I wish I'd done differently. I love my sons with every fiber of my being, but over the years, my priorities fell out of line more than once. Some of these errors in judgment can be blamed on my youth and others stemmed from occasions when I selfishly placed my needs above theirs.

The family dynamic changed numerous times and adjustments weren't always easy. I've agonized over the choices I made that impacted my children in a negative way. In most cases, I was doing the best I knew how at the time, but in hindsight, I wish I'd taken their feelings into consideration more.

No matter how hard I wish for a do-over, there is no way of reliving any of it. The best remedy I could come up with was honesty. I shared my awareness of my shortcomings with my boys. This opened the door to some heartfelt, emotional discussions between us. We were able to clear the air and begin to heal old wounds. Most of it was as hard to hear as it was to say, but we managed to express our individual views.

Aaron and Mark have grown up to be respectful, compassionate, young men with loving hearts which tells me I got something right. After a fair amount of regret and beating myself up, I've reached the point of forgiveness for the times I missed the mark as a parent.

I have offered a sincere apology to my teenage self for allowing those substandard feelings to take root and inflict pain for so many years. It became a poison, a toxic way of life that was endured for far longer than it should've been. That young girl was gracious enough to accept, and since she is me, I am forgiven.

The night Tyger died, I did my best to revive him with chest compressions, but it was too little too late and he was gone. I struggled for a long while with extreme guilt despite the best efforts of the medical professionals and family members who tried to convince me it wasn't my fault. It was crucial that I absolve myself and, over time, I was able to let it go. During the spiritual reading, Tyger confirmed there was nothing I could've done to bring him back and that helped remove my self-inflicted condemnation.

I hold no grudges against anyone who played a role in my past. As with any relationship, there were good times along with the bad. Every memory is now part of the fabric of my life. I have no feelings of ill-will, even toward those who hurt me physically. Holding onto anger or resentment serves no useful purpose. In fact, it becomes a disease, eating away at the soul. If allowed to go unchecked, this festering sore can have a detrimental effect on physical health.

I am not the type of woman to set out to destroy any man or behave in a vindictive manner. My view has always been if it isn't working, it's time to leave. In some instances, the parting wasn't amicable, but over time, it became civil and improved from there. Friendships have been able to develop, which in my opinion, is the ultimate sign of maturity and growth.

I'm strongly opposed to the practice of using children as pawns or objects of manipulation against the other parent. This isn't something I've ever done. The romance may have soured, but the relationships between my sons and their fathers were never made to pay the price. Visits were frequent and I spoke of their dads in a positive light. Even when communication between the adults was difficult, the boys were encouraged to stay in contact. Neither of these men had ever mistreated their sons in any way and were entitled to maintain an active role in their lives.

My forgiveness of others also comes with a genuine desire for their happiness. I feel everyone deserves to know joy in its purest form. We aren't here on this physical journey to live in misery.

The elation Tyger and I introduced into our lives is something everyone should have the privilege of knowing. My wish for all, including my exes, is to know exactly how beautiful the experience is.

Every one of us has fallen short at one time or another. Revisiting those moments and releasing the associated pain is not only cleansing, but necessary. In the process, I discovered despite my tribulations, I haven't become jaded or hardened in any way. Compassion and hope for the future are always present and my faith in the goodness of others is alive and well. I am proud of my perseverance. Although I've endured unimaginable pain and suffering, the capacity to feel remains.

This purging has lifted a weight from my soul. A path has been cleared which enables me to accept and love who I am. Not only during the best of times, but after the occasional stumble, as well. All of it has culminated in me reaching this exact point. Every lesson contributes to the molding of a woman of substance, perfected in her imperfections, and embracing it all.

I describe this stage of my life as "actively healing." I'm on my way to the best I've ever been, but far from the greatest to come.

Chapter Three
Leap of Faith

"**I HAVE ACTUALLY WRITTEN A BOOK.**"

As true as that statement is, there are still moments when it seems unreal. A copy of *Onward into The Light* lies on my nightstand and I marvel at its existence. I consider myself to be rather ordinary, yet I was able to accomplish this extraordinary feat. This quiet, somewhat reserved woman managed to become a published author. How did this come to be? The simple answer is... I believed I could, so I did.

My zodiac sign is Taurus. Although I haven't quite figured out where astrology fits into my acceptance that we are spiritual beings, the personality trait "stubborn as a bull" certainly applies to my character. While completing my first manuscript, I used this indomitable will to my advantage by turning it into determination. I focused on finding answers to every question that came up throughout the writing process.

Completing things on my own is something I find very satisfying, so tasks which seem difficult to some are a welcome challenge to me. There's an old expression, "Necessity is the mother of invention." Well, so is a lack of funds. It's amazing what we can teach ourselves when unable to hire someone to do it for us. This has definitely been the case with me.

When I decided to begin organizing my thoughts, I sat down with a pencil and a composition notepad. As each chapter was completed, I'd get the laptop and type what was written. This worked well because I was able to hear my words again as they were transferred into electronic format. In the process, I could rethink my phraseology, add or delete thoughts, and decide if the message I wanted to convey was clear.

It was great having a sharper version to work with, but I had no idea how to properly format a manuscript. Google became my new best friend. As everyone knows, there is a wealth of knowledge on the Internet. I began doing tons of research on everything; spacing, margins, font size, punctuation, grammar, and even the average word count of a novel. There wasn't one question that went unanswered. I honestly can't recall one resolution that couldn't be located on the worldwide web. As I delved deeper into what goes into creating a manuscript, the lessons learned became as exciting as the content of our story.

When my thoughts turned to creating a cover, I quickly realized hiring a graphic designer wasn't something I could afford. From the beginning, I wanted an image of the sky with sunlight bursting from behind a cloud. Walking across the parking lot at work one day, the blue sky and white, puffy clouds caught my attention. A formation was moving away, revealing bright sunshine, so I pointed my cell phone, camera on, upward and began taking pictures. It wasn't possible to look in the direction where the camera was focused because the rays would have blinded me. I told myself if I kept snapping photos one of them would be perfect. It was true. I'd captured exactly what I needed.

Great, I have the shot, so now what? Back to Google I went for some information on image manipulation and formatting a book cover. Photoshop sounded great, but also expensive so I settled for GIMP (GNU Image Manipulation Program), a free version which has similar features, but is not at all user-friendly. This is where YouTube came in handy. After watching several tutorials on how to utilize the software, I was able to generate a cover which was exactly what I'd envisioned. The best part is, it didn't cost me anything but time and I emerged with a new skill.

While my manuscript was in the final stages of editing, it was time to build a website. Even though I've taken a few courses over the years, the majority of my computer knowledge is self-taught. Honestly, I didn't have the first clue of how to go about designing this, so I did some research and also picked my son's brain for information.

At age eighteen, Mark has grown up in a technological world, so a lot of it was second nature to him. In school, the curriculum was heavily computer-oriented, so he was able to at least answer questions and guide me along. It was a painstaking process, but what a wonderful sense of accomplishment to have my site up and running and be able to say, "I did that." Once again, I have a new ability to show for it.

While my work was in the hands of my editor, Marley Gibson, a best-selling author herself, I anxiously awaited her impression. There was no doubting the power in the subject, but had I been able to express myself clearly? Would my style appeal to readers? I was plagued by questions during the weeks she pored over my labor of love.

There was a huge sigh of relief when Marley reacted with enthusiasm and shared how moved she was by our story. There were minor adjustments to be made and I welcomed her expertise and valuable direction. The tips and advice she gave me on how to improve was explained clearly.

I'm the type of person who prefers to get things right the first time. In the past, this has made it difficult to accept constructive criticism. It isn't that I consider myself perfect; it stems from the disappointment of not "nailing it" the first time out.

Marley did such a wonderful job of explaining the reasons behind the edits she suggested, I reacted with eagerness to make the necessary changes. I have no problem accepting critical views as long as they make good sense. Not only did I re-write various excerpts, but I retained the valuable lessons and continue to apply them. As I create posts for my blog, update the website, and write this book, I am mindful of how to keep readers engaged and which habits to avoid.

Researching and completing so much on my own has given me an advantage. I have an understanding of what is involved in publishing, graphic and web design, video editing, marketing, promoting, and so many aspects of the process. This insight allows me to offer guidance to aspiring authors. By being so hands-on, I have an idea of what a number of services entail. Down the road, when I'm in a financial position to hire professionals in these fields, it will be an informed decision based on what goes into the completion of the project. This will allow me to be an active participant in development and know which questions to ask.

My intent in describing my methods is not to boast in any way. I'm demonstrating how possible it is to do something big with limited resources. It's often a matter of how badly you want it and how much faith you have in yourself to accomplish it. From my perspective, there was no task too great to keep me from getting our story into print.

Sometimes it's about moving out of your own way and just doing it. Rather than come up with a long list of excuses for why it can't be done, direct that energy toward figuring things out for yourself.

It should be obvious from my actions, I did my homework on what goes into writing a book. There is so much information available, literally at our fingertips. A little research can take you a long way; far beyond what you thought you were capable of doing.

Each of us has the ability to achieve whatever we can conceive. The challenge lies in convincing the mind. Once you know what you wish to accomplish, put your plan in motion. Avoid telling yourself it's not the right time. If you adopt that mindset, circumstances will never appear ideal. Believe it will be done and take action to move yourself in the direction of your goal. Worry and doubt are not a part of the equation. As you engage in the process, everything you require will become available just when you need it.

I authored our story based solely on my conviction that it was what I was supposed to do. There was no stressing about where I would find the money to publish or anything else. It was written without doubt of a way being made. My job was to put our journey into writing and the Universe would handle the rest. It was completely out of character for me as I've never been what you'd consider a "chance taker." Yet, I went full steam ahead with this project and the words flowed naturally from my soul.

Sharing my deepest thoughts and personal beliefs has been liberating on many levels. Laying myself bare to the world definitely took a fair amount of courage, but it has also elevated my self-confidence to a level I'd never experienced previously.

There was a point in my grief journey when the thought of merely getting dressed seemed like an insurmountable task. Surviving the next hour hardly seemed possible and making it to another day was practically out of the question. I saw the future as a barren desert; nothing more than a desolate wasteland. There were periods I was stuck and hope was a four-letter word I could not relate to in any way.

Slowly, I began to inch along, painstakingly pulling myself out of the muck and mire of depression. Writing provided an outlet and directed me toward new possibilities. As I became steady on my feet, documenting our love and the effect it had on my life became a goal. The fact that I'd never once considered becoming an author was irrelevant. The decision had been made and it was final. I told myself I was capable of completing this because I was called to do it.

We all have dreams and aspirations and they are completely attainable. There is a misconception that all our ducks need to be in perfect rows in order to even begin—anything. Nothing could be further from the truth. A favorite quote of mine by Dr. Martin Luther King Jr. applies perfectly: "You don't have to see the whole staircase, just take the first step."

Have faith in your ability to make your plans a reality. Believe in yourself with all your heart and soul as you proceed and all will unfold as it should.

How can I be so sure?

I am able to hold the physical manifestation of my goal in my hand and see my name on the cover. I took that first step in faith and slowing down is not an option.

Chapter Four
Heart to Heart

I HAVE BEEN BLESSED with the ability to affect others with my words.

This gift was tucked away, hidden from everyone, including myself. Had it not been for the tragedy of Tyger's passing, this skill may never have been exposed. I'm deeply moved whenever I'm told how relatable my descriptions are to readers. How the story is an inspiration that brings peace to others, is uplifting, and still contributes to my own healing.

As wonderful as this feels, it's still not a cure for the ache that lies deep within.

I've come extremely far from the sullen days following Tyger's transition. My distress is well-managed and the bouts of sadness aren't as frequent. Each smile is genuine and joy has a place in my heart, once again. It probably even appears as though I'm no longer grieving.

Oh, how I wish that were the case. I am always conscious of how different life is without his physical presence. He is always with me—I know that on a soul level. It's a comforting thought, but there are times when I just want to sit and talk with him and hear his responses. I miss my man and it hurts.

After Tyger passed away, I repeated the same questions over and over. Why did he have to go? What did I do to deserve this agony? As I reflect on all that's taken place since, the answers are clear. He had to go because this physical stage of his journey was over. It wasn't designed to punish me, but was actually a defining moment in my own progression. As a result, I emerged with a new level of compassion and empathy for others. This led to our story being told which I know is helping so many other lives. He and I had something important to do and it required us to be on opposite sides of the veil in order to accomplish it.

The logical half of my brain understands and it's such a blessing to be able to help others through their situations by relaying my experiences. Emotionally, I completely accept the truth in the explanation, but it doesn't erase the sadness of missing him. I live conflicted; grateful for the healing effects of sharing, yet still longing to have things as they were.

More than two years after Tyger's death, there was a period of several days when I was feeling down. I couldn't name anything specific that triggered these emotions, but it was a serious case of the blues. As I sat trying to figure out what was wrong, it occurred to me that I missed being a priority in someone's life. It was incredible to know how much he cared about my happiness and the many ways he made me smile. That was gone from my daily routine and I was mourning the loss of knowing I mattered to another person.

That night, Tyger came to see me in a dream. We were sitting together on a bench, so close our legs were touching. I could feel the warmth of his left outer thigh pressed against my right. He was dressed as I'd expect: jeans, his navy blue jacket, and that trademark black baseball cap, the brim turned slightly to the side. Not one word was spoken. The communication was totally non-verbal, more like an exchange of energy. I could feel everything he wanted me to know. There was such adoration in his eyes, a reassurance of how much I mean to him. I was reminded I am loved beyond measure. He called attention to the strength I possess and all I've overcome. I was left knowing there was no need to mourn something I'd never lost.

Opening my eyes on a new day, I recalled his visit the night before. The connection between us had been so strong, so real. His message was clear and the delivery was perfect. The impression made was far more powerful than hearing a human voice. It's difficult to explain because our communication is based on speech. This was a different level; an advanced way of passing along information and there was no possibility of misinterpreting what was being shared. It was a *knowing*, a comprehension that defies explanation. All I can say is it goes way beyond vocal chords and auditory response.

Our loved ones on the other side are aware of what we're dealing with in our life. They are more than willing to help and want us to know we have no reason to ever feel lonely. Once we accept this truth, they can contact us in many ways. Conversely, if we're not ready or unwilling to acknowledge their attempts, those wishes are honored. Tyger knew exactly what I needed and, because I believe so strongly in his ability to reach me, I was able to receive it. He demonstrated how important my happiness still is to him and his desire to see me enjoying life.

Several months after *Onward Into the Light* was published, I had a dream that I was back at the casino (where I used to work). Not as an employee or patron, I appeared to be there visiting friends. Walking down a long hallway with my cousin, Angy, I noticed a dear friend up ahead of us. Her name is Sally and I was so excited to see her because she passed away many years earlier. As Sally approached, I was struck by her appearance. She looked wonderful; so vibrant. I gave her a tight hug and we smiled at one another, though not speaking.

There was much I wanted to ask, but before I had the chance, Sally lifted her chin in a motion, signaling I should turn and look behind me. When I did, no one was there. Puzzled, I looked at her and she repeated the gesture. This time Tyger was rounding the corner and walking toward us. He was almost glowing; healthy and full of life. Our eyes met and we were instantly locked in a loving gaze. Everything came to a halt and time ceased to exist.

I lost myself in the wonder of seeing him; so reminiscent of his human self, only more. He was completely present with added qualities which seemed to strengthen our connection. There was an air of rejoicing as we expressed our mutual admiration. Without saying a word, we let the other know how great it was to be this close again.

Several minutes passed before I remembered I was carrying a copy of our book. Holding it out to him, I expressed in thought, "Look, baby, here it is. This is it." He had the most approving smile on his face and I felt his joy.

Tyger took the book from me and flipped to a blank page near the back. He pulled a pencil from his left shirt pocket and drew a picture of a little girl who I instinctively knew to be my granddaughter, Sophia. Above her head, he added a thought bubble and then pointed to it while nodding his head, "Yes." He was confirming that he communicates through her. It felt like he was saying, "You're right. Keep listening to Soph, I'm talking to her."

Again, there were no words spoken in the dream, it was all energy and feeling. I was ecstatic when I awoke. Not only for seeing Tyger, but my good friend, Sally, as well. She and I had been close friends in our time working together at the casino and she crossed over several years before Tyger. Sally hadn't forgotten me and I was thrilled. I wondered if she'd been able to come through because I was now open to contact from beyond the veil. I could imagine the exact scenario of Tyger saying, "Hey Sal, I'm going to check on Diane tonight. Why don't you come, too? She'll be happy to see you."

All my dreams of Tyger since his passing have had one major component in common. In every one, we are fully aware of his death. He died in the same manner as in real life, but he is alive again and this doesn't feel strange, at all. When he appears, I'm always conscious of how much I've missed him and how difficult it's been during his absence. I manage to relay that to him in some non-verbal manner. It seems I need him to know how hard it's been to go on without his physical presence.

As the dream progresses, this awareness of his death and resurrection stays with me. It raises questions which I've yet to receive answers:

"Where have you been?"

"How did you come back?"

"Why do you look so healthy after dying?"

I never direct these thoughts to him, but they are present in my mind during the entire visit. My curiosity is overpowered by the joy of being close to him again. It's almost like I'm whispering to myself, "Never mind where he's been, enjoy the time you have now."

My subconscious travels to many different places as I sleep. There are mornings where all I can do is scratch my head at the outrageous visions of the night before. I don't consider every dream as having a hidden meaning nor do I feel each one is an attempt by Tyger to communicate. His visits have a distinct clarity about them.

Ordinary dreams have a fuzzy, somewhat disconnected aura. When Tyger makes his nocturnal appearances, it's more like we're meeting in another dimension. It's as though we've both traveled to some neutral ground between worlds. Awareness is heightened and understanding is keen and sharp. It isn't a replaying of events we shared during his physical journey, at all. Fresh experiences are created during these periods, which mean we are still making memories.

I'm able to retain details of the time spent together in this alternate reality, if you will. It's difficult to label our meeting place because it isn't so much a geographical location as it is an incredible sensation. The backdrop is always something familiar (i.e. the casino), but the energy tells me we've transcended space and time. A window is opened and our vibrational alignment makes the connection possible.

This explains why I have no problem accepting his apparent "return from the dead" in each vision. These meetings are intended to demonstrate to me that he never left. The act of acknowledging the shedding of his physical form and ability to appear whole again is a symbolic assurance that there is no end to us, only a transition.

To anyone who hasn't been contacted by a loved one who's crossed over, this probably sounds far-fetched. I'm doing my best to accurately describe what takes place; however, in this case, words fall short. There doesn't seem to be a specific rhyme or reason to these occurrences, either. I've had days that were filled with thoughts of Tyger, yet he didn't show up. On other occasions, he's dropped in while my mind was on a million other things. I suspect it happens when there is the lease amount of resistance. I've certainly tried to "will" him here many times, but that doesn't appear to work. At least not in my case.

If I knew of a secret formula to magically bring our departed to us whenever we asked, I'd be happy to share. The best advice I can offer is to hold on tightly to love. It's the binding agent used to construct the bridge between this world and the next. Allow yourself to grieve, but embrace the moments of relief.

Cherish the reminders that make you smile without feeling guilty because the tears have stopped. Those bursts of joy naturally raise our vibration and it's always easier to establish a connection when that happens.

I've felt the frustration of pleading for a visit or a sign and receiving no response. In those instances, I shift my focus to the love we share and exercise patience. Even if it takes longer than expected to hear from Tyger, I don't doubt our connection. A major component of keeping the lines open is unwavering faith. Messages often don't arrive in the manner we'd expect so we have to remain diligent. It would be great to find a handwritten note, a professing of their undying devotion, lying beside our heads on the pillow. If only it were that simple.

Contact from beyond the veil can pack quite a punch. It's not always as clear as pen and paper, but considering what it takes for the message to reach us, the value is immeasurable. Acknowledge the bond between souls. Feel it with your entire being, regardless of what anyone else says or how long it's been since the last sign or dream visit. Don't think of yourself as unworthy if others receive signs and you're still waiting. Stay open, encouraged, and always speak with confidence knowing they can hear you.

The possibilities of what's available to us are endless. The glimpses I continue to receive of what lies beyond the physical leave me astonished and inspired. The key is to look past what we've been conditioned to accept. Our eyes are not capable of penetrating the illusion of separation between worlds. It requires a view based on faith and love which can only be achieved from within.

The truest definition of a heart to heart.

Chapter Five
A Purpose Revealed

ONE OF THE GREATEST DISCOVERIES we can make is finding our passion. What is it that really drives us to be the best we can be? I've lived the majority of my life maintaining the status quo. If it wasn't broke, I saw no need to go about trying to fix it. I was relatively happy in my complacency; accepting my lot in life and taking the good with the bad. As I reflect on those years, I can't recall feeling overly passionate about anything. Interests came and went, but nothing seemed to have a lasting effect.

Growing up, I did well in school. There was no stress when report cards went out because things came easily to me. In fact, I've had to endure a fair amount of teasing from family members who lovingly refer to me as "Straight 'A' Student." I wouldn't say I took my intelligence for granted, but I don't recall feeling special in any way. It's just the way it was. Even though I didn't quite understand why some seemed to struggle, I never thought my abilities made me superior to anyone else. I was always willing to help others make sense of things.

My parents were extremely proud of my accomplishments, so you can imagine their dismay during my senior year of high school, when I announced I would not be continuing my education by attending college. To say they were disappointed doesn't even begin to cover it. After several failed attempts at changing my mind (that stubborn Taurus nature), it was clear there was no persuading me to rethink my decision.

I'll never forget telling my mother I planned to relax after the end of the school year and enjoy the summer. In September, I'd begin looking for a full-time job. She listened quietly with no response. When I emerged from my bedroom the morning after graduation, she handed me the newspaper. "These are the want-ads," she'd said. "I've circled several that sound like a good fit. Eat and get dressed, you've got a busy day ahead."

That was the end of my aspirations to lounge the next couple of months away. My mother had spoken and she didn't bite her tongue once during the delivery. Her message was received loud and clear. She may not have been able to do anything about my refusal to pursue higher education, but there was no way she'd allow me to bask in leisure. It was either school or work, my two options.

My mom was small in size, standing four foot, ten and three-quarter inches, but she was large in spirit. Despite her appearance, my mother was a tall woman. She was as honest as they come and did not mince words. She was the type of person who commanded the respect of others, only not in a harsh way.

She always spoke from a place of love and there was a wisdom about her that let you know she wasn't blowing smoke.

My father's personality stood in stark contrast to Mom's. He was mild-mannered, funny, and polite to a fault. Interactions with my dad left you feeling glad you'd been graced by his presence. This isn't to imply he was weak in any way. His birth sign was also Taurus and he had quite a temper if anyone was foolish enough to provoke him. There was no chance of me causing any adverse reactions. I'd been a "daddy's girl" since birth and the apple of his eye. You would be hard pressed to find anyone with an unkind word to say about my father.

My parents married in their early thirties and I came along ten months later. They met in New Bedford, my mother's birthplace. After the wedding, they settled in Norwich, Connecticut, my dad's hometown. In our household, Dad worked and Mom stayed home to raise me. Dinner was always at the same time every day and we had a structured routine. I am filled with fond memories of long car rides in the country, picnic dinners at the park, and going out for ice cream in the summer. They came to every school play and event, beaming with pride in the audience.

We didn't have much, but growing up I was completely unaware of this. I never thought of us as poor or anything close to it. We didn't own a house, but our apartments were just as good. There was always food to eat, nice clothes to wear, and a clean, comfortable place to live. When school activities or trips rolled around, I was always allowed to go with spending money in my pocket. Now that I know what it takes to maintain a household,

I'm sure there were plenty of struggles. Neither of them ever hinted at it. They provided for me and my character is defined by the values instilled by them.

Following graduation, I went to work, accepting various entry-level positions before being hired by an area casino which translated into a twenty-year career. Over the course of those two decades, I received several promotions and advanced into a management position. I wouldn't call it my dream job, but it was familiar and comfortable. The bills were being paid and I was providing for my children. I didn't see a need to seek anything further.

Two months before Tyger's passing, that all came to an end when I was let go as a result of restructuring. My position had been eliminated. Due to circumstances beyond my control, major life changes began to take place and there wasn't one thing I could do about it.

Tyger's transition from the physical world sent me into an abyss. In the aftermath, I've become acquainted with my authentic self. As I've already said, the initial act on this journey of self-discovery was writing my first book. Little thought was given to what direction I would take following its release. Of all the possibilities, public speaking seemed the least likely choice for someone like me.

If you were to conduct a poll amongst my family members, asking for the name of their most timid, bashful relative, they would say, "Diane." Whether you approached my mother's side or my father's, you'd receive the same answer without an ounce of hesitation. It's a rare occurrence to find me talking to people I've known all my life, so addressing total strangers was completely out of the question.

If I'd been told ten years ago, *"You're going to write a book and it will touch people in ways you can't even imagine. The strength of your passion will motivate you to get up in front of crowds to speak. You won't be one bit nervous either; in fact, you'll actually look forward to doing it."* I would've told that person they were completely nuts.

Me? Little Diane Santos, write a book **and** speak publicly about it? Never in a million years. Yet, lo and behold, that's exactly what happened.

The first opportunity to speak presented itself at my job in a cardiologist's office. I was relatively new to the position which followed my many years at the casino. The practice is in my hometown owned by Yale New Haven Hospital parent company in New Haven. News of my book made its way up the chain of command, reaching the Vice President of Heart and Vascular. After hearing my story during a visit to our location and learning that Tyger passed as a result of cardiac issues, the Vice President invited me to speak at Yale. Yale! The event was an open forum on the Patient Experience to be attended by leaders and medical personnel.

Tyger had been a patient of another cardiology group in town and I was struck by the difference in levels of care between the two offices. His diagnosis of Congestive Heart Failure came about ten months prior to his death. Beyond an initial consultation with his cardiologist following his discharge from the hospital, he had no additional visits. Individuals with the same disease being seen at our practice had monthly appointments. Because of this, I held the unique position of witnessing the process from both perspectives; as the family member of a cardiac patient and an employee of the hospital.

Given my personality, it would be natural to assume I was nervous about getting up to tell my story publically. Not only was it my first time doing this, I'd be addressing a group of highly-educated people. That should have been intimidating for a small town girl who hadn't even attended one day of college. Instead, my reaction was the total opposite. Rather than apprehension, I felt excitement. I literally could not wait for the day to arrive. There was no need to prepare a speech because I'd lived the story and wanted it to flow naturally. I jotted down some bullet points on index cards to keep me on track, put a couple copies of the book in my purse, and headed off to New Haven.

My manager had a presentation to give first, and then she would announce me to the room. Sitting on the edge of my seat, book in hand, I eagerly awaited my moment. Walking toward the podium, a sense of confidence surged through every vein and artery of my body. This was unlike anything I'd ever known, yet felt right in every way. I was exactly where I was supposed to be.

While speaking, my eyes traveled through the audience. The connection was palpable and the attendees were obviously interested and engaged in what was being said. This added to my comfort level and confirmed I was definitely in my element.

When I reached the end of the program, a woman raised her hand to ask how she could go about getting a copy of my book. She explained her husband's dad had recently passed and her mother-in-law was having a difficult time. Since her family would be going for a visit that weekend, she thought this would bring the grieving woman some peace. As I approached with the copy, she asked to hug me and expressed her gratitude for my willingness to share my experiences.

There were questions from the group which opened a dialogue on how the medical establishment can better educate patients; especially those receiving a new diagnosis as inpatients. As we were leaving, there were numerous requests for my business card. Several expressed their appreciation for our story. I distinctly remember the look of approval in the eyes of the Vice President as he took my hand in both of his to thank me for speaking. It was one of the most sincere handshakes I've ever known.

On a later visit to my workplace, the Executive Director of our department explained to my co-workers how well-received I was in New Haven. She went on to say the audience was enthralled and had left the event with a clearer understanding of what they can do to improve patient care. Her words were followed by a round of applause from the people I work with every day. It was humbling and evoked an emotional response not only from me, but from several others, as well.

My first public speaking engagement hadn't happened just anywhere. It was at a hospital which is part of the prestigious Yale University. Did I mention *Yale?* This is a world-renowned, Ivy League school. The first Ph.D. to be issued in the United States took place at Yale in 1861. The mere mention of the name carries notoriety and is highly respected in academic circles. So, yes... a university steeped in rich history was the venue in which I made my debut. There was good cause for me to feel pressure, yet I had been completely at ease.

Standing in front of a room full of strangers discussing such a personal topic had been like an out-of-body experience. As comfortable as I was, a portion of my brain was saying, "What are you doing? Don't you know you're supposed to be petrified right now?" This was easily ignored because I'd found my niche.

As those questions were whispered, my inner being laughed them off. There was no room for insecurity in that space and I was completely aware of it.

A few months later, an opportunity arose to speak at our local library. A family friend facilitated introductions between the Director of Events and me and after chatting, we settled on a date in early autumn. This would differ from the Yale engagement since it meant addressing a hometown crowd. These were friends and family members of Tyger's and mine. Most of them had read the book, but they were coming to hear it told in person.

Was I worried?

Not at all.

The event was promoted on Facebook and I shared the flyer I'd created; inviting all to attend. The library did their part, as well, posting it on their website and calendar. The director explained how difficult it is to get members of the community to participate, especially with the rise in numbers of self-published authors. They welcomed me and were happy to host my program; however, there wasn't any way of guaranteeing a sizable crowd in attendance.

The day of my talk, I arrived early and set up a display with books, business cards, a printout of book reviews and a floral arrangement I'd made, in calming shades of blue. Since my website now featured a blog, I'd begun asking for subscribers to follow along and provide their email addresses so they could be added to my mailing list. Subscription forms were available which could be completed by anyone who wanted to receive uplifting messages and information.

Guests began filing in and before I knew it, we had to set up extra chairs. I was thrilled and grateful for the incredible turnout. On the podium were the carefully thought out bullet points I'd printed on index cards, yet I barely referred to them. As I spoke, there was a calm assuredness in my tone. When I paused for questions, several people responded. They didn't want to ask anything; instead, they shared how the book had impacted them in a positive way. Once again, the decision to put our story in writing had been validated and it was coming from people who were near and dear to our hearts.

In addition, I have to say, it really doesn't get much better than that. Several copies of the book were purchased that night and I gained multiple subscribers to my site.

The event was recorded, so I was able to review the entire evening. When I played the video back, it was amazing to see how comfortable I was in the setting. Of course, we always find reasons to be critical of ourselves, "I should've said this or I could've done that," but overall I was pleased. My cousin, Marcy, was gracious enough to be the videographer. She told me later how sore her arms were from holding the camera so long.

However, she did a wonderful job capturing everything, including the members of the audience who spoke.

There was forty-five minutes of footage and I wanted it shortened to ten minutes or so. Since I had no idea how to accomplish this, I watched YouTube tutorials on how to operate Windows Live Video Editing Software which was already installed on my laptop. Not only did I figure out how to do it, I also managed to create a much shorter version of my presentation and upload it to my website. This was a huge cost-saving venture and another skill set to add to my repertoire. Don't get me wrong, it was one of the most time-consuming things I've ever attempted, but worth every bit of effort that went into it.

My next event was at the East Lyme Public Library, several towns away. Once again, I advertised by circulating flyers and posted numerous reminders on Facebook. I'd hoped to draw a decent crowd, but wasn't sure if anyone I knew would travel to attend. The library requested attendees to register for the event and I hadn't checked with the director to see if anyone responded. My outlook was that it would turn out well so there was no need to stress over who may or may not show up. Mark and Sophia were going with me, so I was guaranteed at least two guests and friendly faces.

We arrived at the library an hour early. This isn't unusual for me as I'm known in my family for being notoriously early and also for having no patience with those who can't seem to be anywhere on time. I'd never been to this location before, so I'd wanted plenty of time to set up and get a feel for the environment.

The complex was beautiful. In addition to the library, there are senior and youth centers with plenty of activities and the community participates in many of the programs they offer. Mark was driving and, as we entered the lot, I noticed a Cadillac parked on the far left. It was the same model and color as the Cadillac Tyger had driven. The car now belongs to his older brother, so I said, "Look, there's the Caddy. Bob must've come to hear me speak. We'll look for him when we get inside."

We were greeted by the library's assistant director who showed us to the room we'd be using for the afternoon. She told me five people had registered to attend, but the number didn't mean anything since many choose to show up without notice. I was glad to hear of the response and excited to be there. My intent is to share my story with whoever cares to listen so this news was encouraging.

The walls were lined with shelves of historic books and nautical memorabilia stored behind glass doors for protection. The furniture had an antique look, as did the podium I'd be using. The rows of chairs faced the front of the room in a semi-circle formation, an intimate setting for a book discussion. A feeling of comfort washed over me as I acquainted myself with the surroundings.

Sophia helped set up the table with a book display as Mark found the right spot for the camcorder. He was taking his responsibilities of recording the event and capturing photos quite seriously. Part of his motivation may have been the possibility of using my car that evening, depending on his performance at the event. Whatever the reason, I knew he had his part handled.

Around ten minutes before I was scheduled to speak, people started to arrive. Each new face added to the joy I felt by simply being there. After presenting a donated copy of *Onward into The Light* to the staff, I began sharing my experiences. The energy in the air was incredible as I connected with these women I'd never met. This was entirely new, addressing a strange crowd who came to listen because they were interested in the subject and what I'd been through.

Just from their facial expressions and body language, I could tell the ladies were comfortable and relating to my words. We were on the same page. When I asked if there were questions, several shared signs they'd received from loved ones on the other side. One woman told of her husband's fondness for hummingbirds. After his passing, a hummingbird flew into her sunroom (this had never happened while he was alive) and the little bird refused to leave her. She managed to get it onto a patio chair where it stayed for almost thirty minutes before flying off. There was no denying this sign of love and I thanked her for sharing it with the group.

As my talk was coming to an end, Sophia raised her hand and asked to come up to the podium. She whispered, "Nani, tell them about how whenever you got sad, I told you Mike was there with us."

I relayed what she'd said and they loved it. None of them had read my book, so I explained Sophia's significant role in keeping Tyger and me connected. It was touching to see this little girl so eager to share her part in our journey and it was a perfect ending to the afternoon.

When the last of the guests left, Mark and Sophia each grabbed a box and we packed everything up. As we headed toward the exit, I realized we hadn't seen Bob.

"I could've sworn Mike's brother was here. I guess it wasn't him," I said to Mark. "You saw the Caddy when we pulled in, right?"

"Yeah, it was parked on the side," my son answered.

At this point, we were outside and could see the entire lot. The Cadillac was gone.

I mentioned again, "I know I'm not crazy. Did you both see it when we got here?"

This time Sophia responded, "Nani, it was another sign."

Mark and I shot each other a look of surprise, then he said, "I was thinking that, but I didn't say it."

Of course, it was.

It was no accident or coincidence. The owner had driven to the library without the slightest idea their vehicle was being used to deliver a message.

Smiling, I said to the kids, "Wow, I didn't think of it that way, but you're right. This has to be a sign."

"It is Nani," Sophia said. "Mike wanted you to see the car so you'd think about him."

Once again, Tyger had caused one of those in-your-face events to happen. Of Tyger's many possessions, nothing comes close to the deep, emotional response evoked by that gray Cadillac Deville. It was the perfect reminder. Placing it directly in my line of sight filled me with him the second we arrived on the property. This was an assurance of how well it would go, even if I didn't catch the hint until the event was over. I have no doubt his essence was in the room, encouraging me and helping my spirit feel at ease. Tyger definitely had a hand in making the day a success.

This speaking engagement differed from the first two. At Yale, I hadn't known the audience either, but their reason for being there was a meeting. They hadn't come specifically to hear about my life, although they were obviously touched and came away with a new understanding. At my hometown library, the room was filled with family and friends who knew my story and came to show support. The energy had been powerful; brimming with love and a sense of pride. I describe these events as climbing a staircase. Each one is the equivalent of taking the next step.

Sharing my progression in a public forum is my passion, but the exposure *Onward into The Light* continues to receive doesn't stop there.

I've been an invited guest on Blog Talk Radio, a show titled, "Bridge Between Two Worlds." The interview centered on my experiences since Tyger entered the afterlife and our ongoing connection. This was a first for me, as I took calls from listeners and answered questions asked by the host.

Shortly after publishing, my work caught the attention of noted filmmaker and motivational speaker, Reggie Bullock. One of his most successful films, "A War for Your Soul," released in 2009, propelled him into the spotlight and was seen by upwards of ten million viewers worldwide. Reggie is a former resident of Norwich and, although we'd never met, the subject matter appealed to him. He asked to feature my book on his website,

JoyfulToday.com, which focuses on positive, inspirational topics. Honored by his request, I agreed and it remains in the book club section of his site.

I am grateful for every mention and each opportunity to expand my reach. No event is too big or small because my intent is to touch as many people as possible. If even one person is helped through the telling of this incredible odyssey I've embarked on, then it's all worth it to me. My goal has never been the acquisition of praise or accolades, even though I'm deeply humbled by it and highly appreciative. What is most important to me is being able to validate experiences and offer hope to the bereaved. If fulfilling that goal should lead to notoriety, I'd consider that the "cherry on top."

I firmly believe we were born with a natural gift; a special talent that may stay hidden for years until one day it bursts forth. This has certainly been the case with me. Through debilitating pain and sorrow, my true purpose has been revealed. There is no possible way I could've predicted someone like me would someday give a voice to many. Now that I've discovered my calling, there is no holding back.

It makes no difference how long it took to arrive on this path; the point is to continue in the direction it leads.

That's exactly what I intend to do.

Chapter Six
No Distance Between Souls

LEARNING WE CAN CONNECT with our loved ones on the other side has been one of the most gratifying discoveries of my life. At times, it feels similar to interpreting a cryptic language, especially when the message is subtle. Since we often move at a hectic pace, their communications can be missed. After all, they are competing with a multitude of distractions as we go about our daily activities.

Just over two years after Tyger's death, the signs didn't appear as frequently. Other than the occasional dream visit, I wasn't hearing from him. Why had he suddenly become so quiet? Was the problem on my end? Perhaps he was still reaching out, but I wasn't tuned in. The speaking engagements, book marketing, and blog posts were keeping me pretty busy. My nightly conversations with him had gotten much shorter since sleep came faster. Had I cut myself off from receiving? Was he drifting away? I began to consider having another reading, hoping for some answers.

Before I had a chance to decide whether or not to schedule an appointment with a medium, an invitation arrived to attend a class. It was titled, "Connecting to Spirit World" and with a name like that, there was no way I'd miss the opportunity. Not only was the subject intriguing, the timing couldn't have been better. I accepted the invite without hesitation, filled with curious excitement of what the night would bring.

The event was hosted by Laura, the beautiful soul who had connected Tyger and me at the first reading. It had been over a year since that incredible evening which changed me forever. I had no idea what to expect this time, since it wouldn't be a one-on-one setting. Anticipation increased and my outlook was positive as the day drew closer.

I arrived about ten minutes early and immediately felt a sense of calm familiarity come over me as I entered Laura's office, located on the lower level of her home. She greeted me with a hug as she showed me to the stairs.

"Go on up and make yourself comfortable," she said. "Introduce yourself to the ladies. I'll wait down here for the rest and be up in a few."

When I entered the upper level, I was struck by the beautiful décor. The walls were white as was the floor and sheer curtains on the windows. It was such a relaxing atmosphere with soft lighting which filled one with an immediate sense of peace. Soon, more guests arrived and we got acquainted while completing our nametags. Laura invited us to enjoy the many refreshments she had placed on various tables. I don't think I've ever felt more welcome in a room full of strangers.

As we settled in, Laura went over the night's agenda. "I'll read for each of you, one at a time. As the rest listen, jot down any thoughts that pop into your head. Don't worry about it making sense, just write what you're feeling and we'll go over it afterward."

I understood the instruction and cleared my mind as she began the first reading.

It was fascinating to see and feel the reactions as each woman heard messages from a departed one. The love in the air is tangible as souls connect. Being in the presence of such powerful energy brings out so many emotions. Laughter, tears, sadness, joy, the list goes on and on.

My senses were alert as I waited to write down the random words that were sure to manifest. Nothing came. Others were writing and sharing what had come to them. Several listeners' thoughts actually had meaning to the individual who was being read at the time. It was fascinating, but my notepad stayed blank. I didn't seem to be picking up on anything. It was a little discouraging, but soon it was my turn to sit down beside Laura.

The moment of truth had arrived and I was a bit nervous as I rose from my seat with a picture of Tyger in hand.

My silent prayer as I crossed the room. *"Here we go baby, please be here."*

Settling into my spot on the plush sofa, I noted how soft it was and the comfort of the surrounding pillows. My body was instantly at ease as I placed the photo in her hand. Laura looked at Tyger's smile as a matching one formed on her face. She began to speak...

Laura: *He is so happy with you. He says you're his hero and he's proud of you. The book will go further than Amazon and he is saying you will be an inspirational speaker. He's showing me you'll be interviewed by a magazine. It's coming.*

Diane: Wow! That's amazing.

Laura: *He's talking about his life here. Was he in a gang or did he have violence in his past? A lot of fighting?*

Diane: No, I wouldn't say a gang, but he definitely experienced violence and more than his share of fights.

Laura: *Well, he says he is "Prince Charming" now, compared to all of that.* [Laughing] *He's calling himself "Prince Charming." He says when you entered his life he finally got to use his heart. He loves you and he's not going anywhere. There is still much to do together. He's mentioning your children; you had a problem or disagreement recently?*

Diane: Yes, I did, with my oldest son. We had a discussion this morning.

Laura: *He says not to worry about it. Your son will get his shit together.*

Diane: [Laughing] *That's him talking, all right. Those are his words.*

Laura: *Now, he says there's a birthday coming. He wants me to say, "Happy Birthday." Who is that meant for?*

Diane: My youngest son. His birthday is this weekend, on Saturday.

Laura: *Well, he says "Happy Birthday." He's talking about a grandchild. A little girl... he's calling her a princess. I see her in a princess dress. Is this your grandchild?*

Diane: Yes, my granddaughter, Sophia. The two of them were very close. I'm going shopping for a dress for her tomorrow because she's invited to a princess tea party this Sunday.

Laura: *He's talking about your appearance. Have you lost weight? He says you look hot!*

Diane: *Oh my goodness* [Laughing] *that's funny. Definitely him, but still funny.*

Laura: *He mentions how good it is for him there. He says God is good and much bigger than you know. He wants you to know he's happy and loves you very much.*

She ended the reading with a hug and then asked me to tell the group about my book. My voice was a little shaky as the tears fell. I noticed others were emotional also as I explained, "I wrote a book about my grief journey as a way of helping others who have suffered a loss. After Tyger passed, I wanted to die. It wasn't until my first reading with Laura that I found my will to live again. Sharing our story has been therapeutic for me and the book is doing very well. I'm so grateful to be able to help others who are suffering."

I shared the title of the book and the information on where it can be found. Several of the ladies remarked how great it was that I'd been able to direct my pain toward doing something positive and expressed an interest in reading *Onward into The Light*. No matter how many times my accomplishments receive attention, my reaction is always humility. The experience is humbling and I am ever grateful. I thanked them as I returned to my seat.

When the class was over, Laura asked if I'd been able to pick up on anything from the others being read.

"No, I didn't get anything. I kept hoping to have something to write, but my mind was blank. What's wrong with me?" I was laughing as I asked, but still looking for an answer.

"There's nothing wrong with you" she answered. "Just stay open. It will come."

Laura thanked us for being there and, after more hugs, I was in the car making my way home. The ride is a little over twenty minutes, so I had time to process what transpired. I was over-the-moon after hearing from the man I love.

"You're still here, baby. You haven't left me." I thanked him as I drove along on that dark highway. My faith had been restored and the connection reestablished.

Later in the evening, as I relaxed in front of the TV, a thought came to me out of nowhere. Remote in hand, I was flipping through channels when I heard in my mind's ear, "You are a good woman."

There was no one else in the room and it was clearly expressed in my head. It was formatted as a thought, yet I knew it wasn't my doing. Someone had placed it there; a non-verbal communication. There was no doubt of who sent the message. Tyger had spoken those words to me so many times in this life and he knew I needed to hear them again.

One day, I hope to develop the ability to read others as many of the ladies in the class were able to do, but I was there for another reason. My spirit had been drawn to attend in order to strengthen the signal between Tyger and me. The questions I'd been asking about our connection required answers. Those doubts needed to be removed and what better way to do it than by hearing from him directly.

That was my purpose for being there. A demonstration of how close we are; a reminder that this separation is a temporary illusion. Souls don't recognize or even comprehend time and distance. Love is the indestructible bridge and once again, the fog had lifted.

Chapter Seven
Encouraging Occurrences

I THOROUGHLY EMBRACE THE CONCEPT that we are spiritual beings having a temporary human experience.

In my eyes, that is undeniable and not open to debate.

Death is no more than a transition and we continue on, retaining our memories and core personalities. Pride and ego are lost when we shed our physical bodies, but the lessons and knowledge stay with us. As firm as this belief is, my acknowledgment of the rights of others to their views is equal in strength.

The world we live in is full of diversity and contrast. We don't have to look further than our own family and friends to witness many differences in opinions and convictions. Along with that comes various levels of acceptance. There are those who celebrate the privilege of making one's own choices and others who think some spirits are a little too free. It takes a fair amount of courage to be on the leading edge of an idea; to follow the calling of your soul when you know the more conservative types are shaking their heads in disapproval. The good news is if you're brave enough to live your truth, it won't matter one bit what anyone else thinks.

In the process of awakening, my thoughts have become more expansive. The word "coincidence" has been removed from my vocabulary and replaced with "spiritual breadcrumbs." I created this phrase to describe those occurrences we may not immediately understand, but those which serve an absolute purpose in our lives. They often appear as ideas or clues that seemingly come out of nowhere.

There was a day I was thinking of my friend, Lee. She has helped keep Tyger and me connected by delivering messages from him on multiple occasions. It had been quite some time since we'd spoken and I thought, "I have to call Lee. I know she's struggling with finding a job. I have to see how she's doing and if she's found anything yet."

This was my thinking late in the afternoon at work. By the time I got home that evening and into my usual routine, I'd forgot all about making the call.

Arriving for work the next morning, I immediately recalled my thoughts from the day before. I was upset with myself for not following through. As the hours ticked by, Lee was on my mind. Late in the afternoon, I was about to take a short break when who should walk into the office, but Lee. I could hardly believe my eyes.

She explained that she'd been thinking of me and decided to stop in rather than call. The reason for the visit was to tell me about a job she'd started and how happy she was there. As I listened to Lee speak, my eyes filled with tears at this incredible news. After months of no communication between us, we'd picked up on this energy and the connection was made.

Following this, something similar happened with my best friend, Angy. At times, you may hear me refer to her as my cousin since she is both. Our dads were brothers and the two of us have been like sisters since the day she was born. Angy is seven months younger than I am and she finds great joy in pointing that out. She is no doubt thrilled to see this fact immortalized in writing. Yes, Angelina, it's right here in black and white for future generations to see; I am the older one, even if it is only slightly.

Angy's husband, Dewayne, is a phenomenal cook and together they opened a restaurant in town, located just down the road from my job. "Uncle D's Blazin BBQ" features Alabama-style barbecue and an extensive menu designed to whip your taste buds into a frenzy. From Dewayne's famous pulled pork sandwich and fall-off-the-bone ribs to Angy's homemade banana pudding and sweet potato pies, you'll never leave disappointed.

After several months, they decided to expand their reach by offering delivery service. They hoped this would appeal to local businesses that would be likely to place group orders. Since I work at a physician's office, I suggested Angy drop off a few menus for the staff. Most Fridays they order lunch, so there was a chance they might give Uncle D's a try. Angy said she was making up packets of information to pass out in the area, so she would stop by my job on Monday or Tuesday of the following week.

I didn't give much thought to it following our conversation and before I knew it, Thursday had arrived. It was a typical morning, and I was busy on the phone, confirming appointments for the next day. I dialed the next number on the list and as it rang, a thought entered my mind, "I wonder if Angy ever came in with those menus. I'll ask the girls as soon as I finish this call." It was possible I'd missed her since I'd been out with the stomach bug for the first part of the week.

As I waited for the call I was making to be answered, I turned my gaze to the parking lot. A gray van rounded the corner, entering my line of sight.

"Oh my God, is that Angy's van?"

I knew it was, but there was no way this could be happening. How could this possibly be real? The odds of her pulling up in front of the door mere seconds after thinking about her had to be astronomical. I watched in disbelief as she parked, and then quickly approached the entrance, menus in hand.

By the time she reached the waiting room, tears had welled in my eyes and my heart was beating with excitement. I explained my emotional state and she laughed as she said, "I was heading back to the restaurant after a run to the bank. I wasn't planning to come today. When I got to the stop sign, for some reason, I took a left at the last second and came here."

Still bewildered, I told her, "Well, you're gonna have a long life because you were on my mind as you turned that corner. This is crazy."

Although I reacted with surprise, part of me understood. On a deeper level, there was a definite sense that instances of connecting through brain waves aren't rare at all. Events like the ones I'd experienced with Lee and Angy are natural and far more common than perhaps any of us are willing to admit.

This is not a claim of psychic abilities, but I do believe as we become more enlightened, our own awareness becomes fine-tuned. Intuition is heightened and we often develop an ability to "know." There may be no way of justifying this feeling, but on a soul level, we are simply convinced. The effect is we unwittingly pick up on these clues—or breadcrumbs—and they lead us directly to where we need to be.

I no longer feel disappointed about having nothing written on my paper from that night during Laura's class. Perhaps reading others isn't within my scope of capabilities at this time while communicating through spirit clearly is. I may not be able to explain the inner workings, but on two separate occasions, I witnessed the power of these silent transmissions. I'm convinced of how real they are.

I am well aware of people close to me who are surprised and may even be slightly leery of my views on spirituality and what happens when we die. Rather than express their disagreement verbally, it's most often conveyed by what is *not* said. In other words, they simply will not discuss the topic. In face-to-face conversations, I quickly pick up on their comfort level by the energy being emitted. This isn't upsetting to me in any way. It's a signal to tread lightly and avoid delving into the intricacies of communicating with the other side.

A long-time friend asked about the meaning behind the title of my first book. I explained *Onward into The Light* represents Tyger's journey since his passing and mine, as well. The "light" references my discovery that death is only a change of worlds; a return to our true origin, or Heaven, if you will. We are much more than these vessels we inhabit and Tyger has proven this by continuing to communicate.

The conversation was in text format via Facebook messenger. Following my explanation, I did not receive a response. This could've been for any number of reasons, but I wondered if he'd been put off by my words. It wouldn't be the first time it had happened, so I left well enough alone and went about my day.

Later that week, I heard from him again. He admitted my subject matter threw him off at first. He'd chosen to stay quiet because his beliefs are different and he didn't want to appear to be discrediting what I'd said. His hope was he hadn't offended me by his reaction.

There was no offense taken, whatsoever.

I replied. "No, not at all. We are each following our own paths, so my truth may differ from yours and vice versa. There is no reason for anyone to be insulted by this because we are here to love one another, not judge."

It is entirely possible to have different views and still respect each other. I feel no need to condemn anyone for what they hold true.

As life progresses, death is a natural occurrence. My desire is to console the bereaved, but only in accordance with their *personal* comfort level. Some religions teach their followers that our departed ones remain out of our reach until called by a Higher Power to rise again. While I disagree, it's not my place to add to their pain by trying to disprove this. Not everyone is ready for the message, so attempting to convince them would be pointless. As an alternative, my approach is to gently remind them that the power of love binds souls together and love never dies.

While I would never impose my opinion on another, if asked directly, I would absolutely state my feelings. Respect for conflicting beliefs is one thing, but denying one's own is an entirely different matter.

My heart aches for those suffering through the sting of grief since I know it so well. Regardless of anyone's thoughts on what happens when we die, it is clear that it hurts those left behind. In time, we learn to adapt to their absence, to some extent, but we never actually get over it. Peace is found in knowing our loved ones still exist, which means my prayer is for an increase in expansive thinking.

A shift appears to be taking place in overall consciousness and individuals, like me, offer guidance by lighting the way for others. There aren't any gimmicks or sales pitches involved. It's a matter of leading by example.

Many are aware of how devastated I was by Tyger's passing, yet now they see the change that has taken place in my being. Possibly this will lead to curiosity as to how I was able to find my way out of the darkness. I am willing to share the healing effects of looking beyond traditional teachings. If the individual is open to these concepts, that's wonderful. For those who aren't ready, it's perfectly fine.

So much energy is spent trying to convert others to believe a certain way. The wars and bloodshed that have plagued our history should be reason enough to adopt a more tolerant way of being. I choose to break this pattern through a commitment to simply live and let live. We should respect our differences rather than point accusatory fingers at one another because we don't pray, eat, think, act, or look the same. No need to insist anyone walk your path; each one has been designed to the specifications of the traveler.

Every soul on this physical journey is a work in progress. There is no one-size-fits-all method to be followed. As we experience the wonder of our personal unfolding processes, the highest expression of love is to allow others to do the same.

Chapter Eight
Forward Motion

THE THERAPEUTIC EFFECT of sharing our story with others is immeasurable. Each time I hear an account of how much the book helped someone, it advances my healing. Somehow, it seems to mend the hole in my heart to know I'm not alone on a deserted island. There are souls out there who know where I'm coming from, even if the circumstances aren't exactly the same. I draw an incredible amount of strength from the reciprocation of love between myself and those of like mind. It gives me a sense of belonging.

Feeling more like a functioning member of society prompted me to consider making a few changes. Maybe it was time to let go of some items and a few practices that had become habit since Tyger's passing. The ritual of smelling his T-shirt, hat, and hairbrush at bedtime was now a robotic function. It was part of a routine, but the sentimental value had faded. Getting into bed after skipping this for the first time was my test.

"How do I feel? Is there any guilt? Does it seem like something's missing?"

My answer was "no" to each question.

"All right, I survived that step without any negative results so I must be on the right track."

That was my thinking as I pondered my next move.

Looking around my room, I focused on the multitude of his belongings I had placed here and there. His slippers under the chair, hats hanging on the wicker room divider in the far corner, and the boxes of clothes, still sitting exactly where I'd placed them after we emptied his apartment, over two years before. I wasn't ready to get rid of anything, but perhaps it didn't need to be so visible.

There were no tears or sadness as I packed several things into a container, including several framed photos of Tyger and me. The shrine I'd built following his death had brought so much peace when it was desperately needed. My ease in moving these items out of view was proof of how far I'd come from in my grief journey. Those deep, dark places were becoming a distant memory. While I still remember the pain vividly, it was manageable now and no longer debilitating.

I placed the box in the back of my closet, along with the large picture of Tyger on a foam poster board, which had been displayed at his service. The white border around his image was full of sentiments, written by friends and family who attended. By now, I had most of the words memorized, having read them so many times.

Lying in bed that night, slowly looking around, I felt lighter somehow. It was as if a portion of the weight I'd been carrying was lifted. My favorite photo of us still hung on the wall above my nightstand, so his smile was there to reassure me each time I turned to my left. Several containers of personal items were across the room; comforting reminders of our time together. In no way did I feel like he was being erased or forgotten. I had found balance.

A by-product of the pain I've endured is an ever-present awareness of my emotions. As the holidays approached, it marked the third season without my love by my side. The heartache I'd known in the two preceding years had diminished significantly. There was a touch of sadness but the sense of dread was gone and my excitement was genuine. I've always enjoyed the atmosphere of the season and it was wonderful to be able to welcome it with open arms.

I prepared our Thanksgiving meal and enjoyed it with my sons, Aaron and Mark along with my precious granddaughter, Sophia. During the prayer, I expressed gratitude for all of them and for the love of family. I also gave thanks for Tyger's presence and my ability to feel him with me in all I do.

The four of us hadn't eaten together for some time, so it was nice to talk and laugh with one another. I marveled at how great it was to be completely there, in the moment. There was no part of me drifting away in sadness. I cleared the table when we finished and got ready to head over to a cousin's house. She had purchased a new home and the family was gathering there for dinner. I'd been invited, but since I'd planned to cook, I told her I'd stop by later in the day.

What an incredible time we had. Everyone kept trying to feed me, completely ignoring my pleas for mercy since I'd just stuffed myself before arriving. Finally, I grabbed a small bowl of salad hoping to satisfy everyone. In my family, it's pretty much non-negotiable. If there's food, you have some. Period. After the meal we laughed, danced and reminisced. I had a great time.

The following night was another gathering of cousins. Plenty of food, drinks, music, and fun. As the evening went on my spirit felt light and happy. I was consciously aware of my joy and the lack of sadness which was present during the previous holiday season. I remembered the year before, how my longing for Tyger had stayed just below the surface. Outwardly, I'd appeared fine, but there was a low-frequency vibration of pain, resonating within. Now, it was noticeably absent and I had no desire to question why. I embraced the sense of calm and enjoyed myself.

I felt I'd turned a corner. Not only had I been able to pack up many of his belongings, I was also experiencing genuine happiness for the first holiday season since his passing. The best part was feeling no sense of betrayal. The process was occurring naturally, so there wasn't a need to punish me or question any of it. The time had simply come to loosen my tight grip on the past and inch my way forward.

A few days following the Thanksgiving festivities, I was tidying up my room. Walking past the cartons of Tyger's clothes that remained in the corner, I wondered if his shirt still held his scent. It had been four months since I'd stopped my nightly ritual, so I was curious.

I removed the large white T-shirt from the box. It was cold to the touch, having been so close to the floor in my old, drafty house. Raising it slowly, I closed my eyes and drew a breath, then exhaled fully before pressing the garment against my face. Immediately, I felt it's coolness as I inhaled deeply, through the nose.

Instantaneously, I was struck by a familiar aroma. The man I love, my Tyger, still lingered in this cold, lifeless fabric. The smell of him wafted into my chest, before coming to rest in the center of my heart. My eyes were squeezed tightly shut, and every muscle in my body grew tense and seemed to freeze. I was completely incapable of moving any extremity.

Internally was another story. My nervous system had sprung into action and every nerve ending was stimulated. I'm not sure I've ever known anything remotely close to this sensation of being paralyzed on the outside while a flurry of chaotic activity was taking place on the inside. My attention shifted to my head, which had become light and dizzy. I realized I'd been holding my breath so I quickly took in some air. The breathing was a release and I was able to move again.

Slowly, I folded his shirt and placed it neatly in its usual place. Walking from my room, still overcome by what transpired, I paused by the dining room table. Without warning a flood of tears burst forth suddenly. Loud, uncontrollable sobs, deep moans coming from my soul. An agony from long ago, reminiscent of the pain which immediately followed the doctor's words that Tyger hadn't made it. I gripped the back of a chair to keep myself from dropping to the floor.

It was a Sunday afternoon, so both my sons were at work. Being home alone, there was no need to suppress anything or keep my voice down. I began speaking to Tyger, through my cries.

"Where are you, baby? I miss you so much and this hurts. I'm hurting, baby, without you here and I need you so badly. I want you to come back; please come back and hold me. I can't do this anymore. I just can't."

After several minutes, I regained control of my emotions and began to process what had taken place. For all my progress, it was evident how little had actually changed. The heartache was raw and real; even after being tucked away. It was still there, waiting for the right trigger, the exact moment to spring forth and remind me of how difficult it is to exist in the physical world without my man. A wake-up call I never saw coming had demonstrated how vulnerable I still am, and on some level, may always be. Once again, grief displayed its power and caused me to sit up and pay attention.

I gained a new understanding from this experience. Regardless of how much time passes or my willingness to let go, missing Tyger is a permanent part of who I am. It has attached itself to the cells of my body and aligned with my soul. There is no escape and I can be rendered helpless whenever it chooses to surface. I accept this truth and while I refuse to allow it to impede my future, it has definitely earned my respect. An important lesson learned as I forge ahead.

Acknowledging how much I miss him is not a sign of regression., It's proof of our connection and is fueled by the purest love. Rather than view these bouts of sadness as something to endure, I see them as opportunities to grow. I will do just that, as I continue my progression. Forward ever, backward never are the words I live by. Carrying sweet memories, each step of the way.

Chapter Nine
Unshakable Foundation

A PHRASE I OFTEN HEAR IS, "You are a strong lady, Diane."

For a good while after Tyger's passing, I completely disagreed with that statement. As time goes on, I find myself assessing the road behind me and I've concluded it did require a fair amount of strength to make it this far. But where did it come from?

I've gone through more trials than some, but not as many as others. Leading up to the life-altering effects of grief, I can't put my finger on anything remarkable enough to explain the source of this resilience. By nature, I'm determined and fiercely independent; neither of those traits had been enough to keep me from pleading with God to end my life. Yet, somehow I was able to escape the darkness.

There are two major components which held the key to releasing me from the clutches of despair. The first was discovering death is no more than a grand illusion. Receiving conclusive proof of the afterlife during my initial spiritual reading put me back on the path to life. It became the catalyst for my heightened awareness and expansive way of viewing everything.

The second was learning about the Law of Attraction and adopting its principles. As I delved deeper into the inner workings of the Universe, I was struck by the simplicity of it. We are made of energy and attract to ourselves what we focus on most. In order to have pleasant experiences, our thoughts must be positive.

Once I accepted in my heart that there is no separation between our souls and those who have crossed over, it filled me with hope. This sent a direct signal outward and more reasons to be hopeful were attracted back to me. I began establishing a foundation based on good feelings which became a platform to build on.

There is a perception in some circles that a belief in this Universal law is a denial of the existence of God. I disagree. I believe we are all connected and part of something much bigger than what we're aware of in this physical form. I fully acknowledge the existence of a point of origin, a higher power if you will, which we are all extensions of. You can call it whatever makes you most comfortable, God, Source, the Universe, the label makes no difference at all. To me, they have the same meaning.

Despite my Christian upbringing, I am in no way religious. Over the centuries, religion has been used as a method of controlling the masses and manipulating minds into doing someone else's bidding. My belief is in Love; living, spreading, and sharing it with others. Mankind has had a heavy influence on religious teachings, but if you strip that away, the ideals of each sect are remarkably similar. Love, faith, and gratitude are the cornerstones; the very concepts on which the Law of Attraction operates.

This common thread indicates the validity of Universal law. The principles are the base, which at some point became distorted by ritual and threats of punishment for failing to follow. The verbiage in the Bible consistently directs the reader to ask in faith, to believe what we ask for is ours. We are told to be grateful in all things, to "do unto others as you'd have done unto you." The parallels in these key points serve as confirmation. The gift isn't about the wrappings, it's what's inside that counts. The label is just a brightly-colored distraction; the power lies in the message.

I choose not to participate in organized religion or to attend church regularly. This is a personal decision I've made, based on my belief system. In no way do I think badly or intend to shed a negative light on those who feel differently. There is an undeniable spiritual connection when like-minded souls come together on one accord, whether it be in a church, mosque, synagogue, or in the privacy of our own homes. Prayer is a powerful manifesting tool, as we send our thoughts and desires into the Universe, to God, or Source. Whether we pray for ourselves or on behalf of others, the signal sets an intent and begins the process of manifestation.

Christianity, Buddhism, and Islam are three of the world's major religions. Their philosophies are based on ideals held by great visionaries whose words were powerful enough to attract expansive followings. It's unfortunate that over time, the emphasis became the method of worship, rather than the content of the message. Jesus was not a Christian; Buddha was not a Buddhist; and Muhammad was not a Muslim. They were highly influential teachers who taught love. The human emotions of pride and ego created walls of separation in man's desire to be right. I find it doubtful this was the intent of these three enlightened souls. Their desire was to inspire unity.

I don't profess to be an expert on religion, nor do I wish to offend anyone. Reading is enjoyable to me and, in my quest for spiritual knowledge, I've come across numerous theological views. An excerpt I found particularly interesting was a comparison of the core ideology of nine sects, spanning the globe. Each one, with slight variations in wording, instructs followers to "treat others the way you would like to be treated." Clearly, a uniform message of love.

Rather than debate the nuances of different faiths, time would be better spent, and the greater good served, by accentuating the similarities. If the commonalities were magnified, there would be less division and a far more united front.

The process of drawing our desires to us is so simple that many feel it can't possibly work, yet it does. Since we are energy, everything is about vibration. Once a decision is made on what we want, it then becomes a matter of alignment. Speaking it creates a vibrational version of that desire. Our behavior from that point on determines how quickly it manifests physically.

The power of gratitude cannot be over-emphasized. Speaking for myself, this is the easiest part of the process. By staying grateful for what we already have, we attract more to be grateful for. We often show thanks for big events, but neglect the small things that make life comfortable.

A useful tool for me is my "gratitude journal." It's a small pink notebook, about three inches wide by four inches long, and each morning I fill one page with what I'm thankful for. Sometimes it's as simple as the restful sleep I had the night before or the delicious cup of coffee I just finished. The subject doesn't matter, it's about acknowledging the pleasure it brought to my life and my appreciation of it.

This act sets the tone for the day. How can we feel anything negative after listing all the bright spots in our lives? It's impossible. Positive emotions raise our vibration and align us with our desires. I have witnessed this process work numerous times so I'm speaking from experience. I'll share a few amazing examples of how my own life experience continues to be enhanced by maintaining this alignment.

I mentioned to a co-worker how nice it would be to go home to meal already prepared. This really isn't a possibility for me, since I do the cooking. Usually, I get in and make myself something small. It's never anything fancy, but I'm always glad to have it, regardless.

Later that evening, I was watching TV thinking I should really get up and throw a meal together. Just then, my son Aaron walked in with a pizza. He was happy to share so there was no need to cook.

The following afternoon, I noticed a missed call from my son, Mark. He was at work, so I dialed back a few minutes later.

He picked up the phone in his usual way, "Hey Mom." He starts every phone conversation with me exactly the same.

I responded, "Hey son, you called?"

"Oh yeah, when I got here I found out I wasn't scheduled. What do you want to eat? I'm going home, so it'll be there when you get in."

A smile spread across my face, a mile wide. This was incredible. He's a thoughtful young man but had never done this before. All of a sudden, the day after I uttered this thought of having a meal waiting for me, he happened to make this generous offer. Coincidence? Absolutely not. Spiritual breadcrumb is what it's called. I spoke and the Universe responded. My gratitude each day for whatever I had to eat was steadily increasing my vibration. It reached such a high level that my desire manifested quickly.

The continued outpouring of support for my book is another example of the Law of Attraction at work. My sole intent in penning our story was to help others and I overflow with gratitude for the love Tyger and I share. The ongoing success is part of the unfolding process and continues to gain momentum.

Disappointment is something I rarely feel. This is a direct result of my determination to focus on the good news and view everything else as a lesson. The effects of this were felt in a big way, following the speaking event at the East Lyme Public Library.

In an earlier chapter, I shared what a wonderful day it was and how engaged the ladies who attended were. During my closing remarks, I announced copies of my book were available for purchase. Additionally, I pointed out my business cards, informational flyers, and subscription forms to join my mailing list. Several guests went over to the table and retrieved the literature, but no one seemed interested in making a purchase.

On our way to the car, I said to my son, "Today was great! Didn't make any sales, but I don't even care about that. The conversation and stories those women were comfortable enough to share lets me know I connected with them. My words and the subject held their interest and they enjoyed listening. Their willingness to participate more than makes up for not selling any copies."

I wasn't the least bit discouraged by the fact that I returned home with the same number of books I'd left with.

Less than three weeks later, I was contacted by a relative. Other than the occasional comment on one another's Facebook posts, there is almost no communication between us. I was understandably surprised to find a personal message from him and when I read it I could hardly believe my eyes.

"Diane, I am going to Connecticut on Saturday. I would like to stop on my way home to purchase five copies of your book. The time will probably be late afternoon. Will that work for you?"

Excited, I typed my response. "Oh my goodness, thank you so much. Yes, I'll be around all day Saturday. I'll forward my number so we can coordinate. Look forward to seeing you."

It only took a few seconds before I realized what was taking place. The Universe was responding to my gratitude for the outcome of the recent speaking date at the library. These sales were a direct result of my positive response and the absence of negativity. Because my focus centered on how well the day had gone without any feelings of lack, this abundance had been attracted to me.

We met as planned and he explained his need for five books. One for himself, a copy for each of his three siblings, and the last would be a birthday gift for a friend whose husband passed away two years prior. He felt my experiences would bring her comfort. As I inscribed everyone with a personal message, my heart overflowed with thankfulness. There was such clarity in my understanding of the steps that had led to this exact moment.

Gratitude is always the key.

As I witness these events in my life, it fuels my confidence and motivates me to reach higher. There is a fair amount of work involved in pursuing any goal, but my approach is from a place of joy and nothing is done grudgingly. This mindset keeps me in alignment with my higher self. The emotions attached to my actions at any given moment are the best indicators as to whether or not I'm on course. Any type of struggle or sense of dread is a signal that I've veered off.

The path to our desires is the one with least resistance. It is paved with anticipation and ease of effort. I am in tune with my inner guidance system as I push forward. Each new challenge is welcomed with excitement, an absolute assurance of moving in the right direction.

Forging ahead with no sense of fear is not only exhilarating but also highly empowering. A wealth of limitless strength has been discovered by living my truth. There was a time

I didn't think I had it in me, but I'm forever grateful to know it's there. Reflecting on the events which led me to this point, I can come to only one conclusion... I am a strong lady.

Chapter Ten
An Open Book

IF ASKED TO DESCRIBE MYSELF in one sentence, it would be, "What you see is what you get." The only person I know how to be, is me. I've never been one to behave a certain way with a particular group then act differently in the company of others. Obviously, I'm more relaxed around those I've known a while than with a new acquaintance, but my basic demeanor doesn't change.

Pouring my deepest emotions into my books is the ultimate statement of transparency and done without hesitation. My desire to help others requires a telling of the whole story. It's not only about my grief journey, but also involves who I was before tragedy struck, which traits were altered and how many remained the same. It means getting down to the depths of who I am in order to explain how I've been able to embrace life again.

Baring my soul is done without hesitation because I wear no false faces. I am not driven by a need to impress or outdo anyone. My goal each day is to simply be a better person than the day before.

I have flaws and shortcomings like everyone else and perfection is not something I seek. The contrast we experience by the occasional fall results in growth. Each stumble is an opportunity to learn, so I look for the lesson. It's not always obvious and sometimes takes a while to present itself, but it's always there. What I'm saying is I accept who I am and feel comfortable in my own skin.

The risk of being so forthcoming is assuming the same is true of those I interact with. Due to my lack of malicious thoughts, I'm caught by surprise when they're directed toward me. This was the case at work when I was accused of speaking negatively about another. It wouldn't have bothered me if it hadn't happened before, but this was the third time in the nearly two years I'd been there that I was being questioned about allegedly saying something hurtful regarding a co-worker.

The accusation wasn't true as had been the case on both preceding occasions. The most difficult part was suddenly finding myself in unfamiliar territory. The initial shock turned to anger, then sadness. I certainly have my share of faults, but being mean-spirited and vindictive are not on the list. My mind simply does not work that way. I've encountered individuals over the years who seem to think pointing out the weak spots of others somehow makes their light shine brighter. Could this be the case here? It's difficult to decipher motives that differ so much from your own.

For reasons unknown, someone seemed to be trying to make me into a villain or a troublemaker. I couldn't, for the life of me, figure out why. I arrive each morning with a smile, overflowing with positive energy. I'm willing to help anyone with anything, yet a perception had sprung up somewhere in that office of me being a problem. Where had it originated?

I replayed conversations and interactions in my mind, trying to determine where this was stemming from, but was coming up empty. I began to feel frustrated when I recalled Tyger's words to me, "Diane, not everyone thinks the same as you do." As I considered his words, I concluded there was no point in wasting time attempting to make sense of this. For reasons I may never understand, there are some who operate based on hidden agendas. Maybe I had mistaken a work relationship for friendship or unknowingly offended someone. I could either continue being pulled into this storm or retreat into a place of calm. I decided on the latter.

The bottom line is we cannot control the actions of others. The power lies in our reactions. Once I let go of the need to figure out why this was happening and went back to acknowledging my good intentions, the energy shifted into a positive light. I refuse to allow anyone to steal my joy, even though I have become slightly guarded in conversations as a result. This has been chalked up as a lesson learned and the development of a new awareness.

I've had to accept not everything is deserving of my attention. Each day, we are bombarded with information and not all of it is pleasant. Televisions, newspapers, the Internet, and opinions of others can be draining. The best course of action is to become good at putting our own peace of mind above everything else. Sounds a bit selfish, right? It is and I've discovered that's a good thing.

By making my personal happiness a priority, I've become better equipped to navigate through any waves of negativity flowing in my direction. Rather than develop ways of defending myself against it, I simply choose to acknowledge my sense of well-being regardless of the conditions. This is what it means to be unconditionally happy.

There is much to be said for living with this mindset. Despite my awareness of the correlation between positive thinking and elevated vibrational energy, the effects sometimes catch me off guard. This was the case on a routine trip to a medical facility.

I prefer to make appointments bright and early so my entire day isn't impacted. I'd scheduled some testing for 8:00 a.m., arriving fifteen minutes early for registration. I checked in and took a seat in the waiting room. A few people were there already, so I expected them to be taken in ahead of me. Rather than dig through the pile of magazines on the table, I pulled my phone from my purse to scroll through Facebook.

This is always a good way to kill time. I was aware of people coming and going, but wasn't paying attention to how many minutes had passed. Social media has that effect, which is why it's a good distraction whenever I have to wait for anything. Before I knew it, half an hour had passed.

"This is strange" I thought to myself. "They're normally right on schedule. I'm sure she told me to sit in this area. Did they forget about me? Could I be in the wrong place?"

As I finished this thought, I saw a woman in scrubs walking toward me. "Oh, okay. She's definitely coming for me." She smiled as we made eye contact, but she called another name. There had to be a problem.

I stood and showed her the paper I'd been given as I explained, "My appointment was at eight and I've been waiting quite a while. Am I in the right area?"

She read what I'd handed her and replied, "Yes, you are. Would you like me to check with the front desk for you?"

"No, thank you," I said politely. "I'll go out and speak with them."

I approached the young lady who had registered me forty-five minutes prior. "Excuse me, I was scheduled for eight o'clock, but they haven't taken me in yet. Is there a problem?"

She took the form from my hand and searching her computer for information. After a few seconds and a phone call, she assured me someone would be right out.

Returning to my seat, I noticed a flutter of activity and it was obvious the staff was scurrying to get me in. The other folks in the waiting room overheard my inquiry about the delay and began asking questions.

"How long have you been here?"

I turned to the woman on my left and answered, "About an hour now. I'm not sure what happened, but I think they're getting things ready for me now."

Sure enough, a few seconds later, I heard my name. A low-level cheer erupted from those who'd overheard my dilemma, sharing in my relief. I'm sure there was also a fair amount of concern about having a long wait themselves.

The medical assistant escorting me apologized profusely. "I am so sorry for your long wait today. We had paperwork issues and it was a complete oversight on our part."

I assured her it was quite all right. "No problem, I understand these things happen. I was beginning to think maybe I was in the wrong place and someone was looking for me in another waiting area."

Again she expressed remorse. "Oh no, the mistake was on our part. This should not happen and we don't enjoy making patients wait." Her tone impressed me, so genuine and heartfelt.

I repeated my earlier sentiments. "It's perfectly fine. You're not keeping me from anything. At least, I have the day off."

She smiled and replied, "Well that's nice, but you certainly don't want to spend all of it here with us."

As she went about her work, we engaged in polite conversation. It wasn't long before she had finished. "You can get dressed, I'll be right back."

She stepped out and as I gathered my things, I began thinking about the rest of my day. Originally, I'd planned to go straight to the park for a walk, but hadn't anticipated a delay. My stomach was reminding me I'd skipped breakfast, so my thoughts turned to food.

When she returned to show me out, I noticed what appeared to be a gift bag in her hand. She held it out to me and said, "This is from all of us for the inconvenience of having to wait so long. Thank you for being so gracious."

I paused for a second before responding, wondering if I'd heard her correctly. "Really? Oh my goodness, you didn't have to do that. It was no trouble at all. My day is wide open so you weren't keeping me from anything. Thank you so much."

I made my way through the building, somewhat bewildered by what transpired. Did this actually happen? Did these complete strangers give me a gift?

Stepping outside, I was greeted by the cold, January air as I rushed to get in the car. Quickly starting the engine, I activated the switch that heats the seat. The suspense was taking over and I needed to know what was in the bag. Inside was a semi-tall, rectangular box with beautiful artwork on the exterior. It was a cheerful print, a tan background with golden sunflowers, bright orange chrysanthemums, pale bluish-white sparrows, and black and yellow bumble bees. "Wow," I marveled, "I'd be happy with the box alone."

I removed the cover and inside was a ceramic mug, decorated with the same print as the box. It came with a dark brown, plastic travel lid. The high quality was evident not only in the design but the weight, as well. It clearly wasn't made from low-grade material. As I held it in my hand, I wondered if Tyger hadn't played a small role in all of this. We both enjoyed coffee and he had given me numerous mugs over the years. There is no way this happened by chance. First of all, I no longer believe in coincidences and second, that box could have contained anything.

What are the odds of it being something that held such meaning for us? I was blown away by the gesture.

Replaying the events that led to me receiving such a wonderful token of appreciation, I took note of the tranquility in my spirit through it all. There was never a point where I felt anger or frustration. I accepted the explanation and apologies without harboring any ill will toward those involved. As a direct result, this vibrational match to my positive energy had manifested in the form of a gift. Since Tyger stays close, I believe he saw an opportunity to make his presence felt. He whispered a suggestion on what to give, knowing I would recognize his influence.

What an amazing display of the Law of Attraction at work. Simply put, we get back what we put out. Rather than looking for someone to blame, I was completely at ease. In the grand scheme of things, one hour of time is minuscule. Viewing the situation from that perspective, I saw no cause for anger.

I've always struggled to understand why some individuals feel it's acceptable to show blatant disrespect. I can certainly understand the gratitude the staff felt for my lack of frustration. As an employee of a physician's office, I'm all too familiar with how rude patients can become at times. There are some who don't hesitate to lash out even if circumstances are out of the control of the staff.

Having spent twenty years employed in food service, poor customer behavior is something I know well. My approach has always been to meet their harsh words with kindness. The nastier they become, the nicer I get. It doesn't always improve their mood, but eventually, they give up. I escape the encounter without being drawn into a negative space.

I do my best to limit time spent with individuals who seem to have a problem for every solution. I'm responsible for my vibration just as we all are. For every dark side, there's a bright one and each of us makes a conscious decision on how we view things. I prefer to focus on what's going well no matter how circumstances appear. When I direct my attention toward supportive people, the Universe responds by placing individuals with similar ideals in my path.

As unfortunate as it is, there will always be those who constantly find fault. Their scorn originates from what's lacking in their own lives. It actually has little, if anything, to do with the other person. This energy could be put to better use if directed toward building them up, rather than attempt to tear another down. Each soul will come to realize this in their own time. We are all at varying stages of our journeys.

I genuinely enjoy interacting with others. The eye contact, conversation, coaxing a smile from someone, who, at first glance, doesn't appear to be in a great mood, etc. Establishing connections and exchanging energy is wonderful. Of course, we all encounter the occasional gloomy soul, but we don't have to allow them to bring us down. Despite my timidity during childhood, I've grown into quite a "people person" and I extend the same courtesies to all.

As the saying goes, I was raised to treat the CEO with the same respect as the janitor. We are defined by character, not status. A degree or an astronomical salary aren't qualifiers for special treatment. Integrity and class are traits money can't buy. There are some at the highest levels who have their heads in the clouds and others who are as down to earth as they come. You can also find people doing what society has labeled "menial tasks," yet they carry themselves with grace and could go head-to-head in a conversation with any top executive. By being kind, I have no worries of offending someone who holds an impressive title.

Social standing does not determine my view of others. There is no way of knowing the circumstances that led them to the position they are currently in. I treat everyone with dignity and am simply myself. This ensures I never have to make adjustments, regardless of who enters the room. A respectful approach is appropriate for anyone.

My hunger for acquiring knowledge continues to grow and a major part of my quest involves self-realization. Who is Diane Santos? She's a woman with a heart full of love, gratitude, and good intentions, living entirely in the moment. What drives her? The notion that no matter how much she learns, there is always more to discover.

I've barely scratched the surface on the vastness of the Universe and the power we possess as infinite beings. I'm aware my beliefs may be a bit much for some and that's okay. As my awakening progresses, I have a responsibility to share my truth and inspire others to do the same. The best way to accomplish this is by being open, honest, and unapologetically me.

Chapter Eleven
Tangible Reminders

IN OUR BUSY DAY-TO-DAY LIVES, we often lose sight of the fact that we are actively making memories. There is much I try to recall from when my boys were little. Why hadn't I paid closer attention? I failed to realize there would come a day when I'd want to replay those events. There never seemed to be enough time because life happens so fast.

I've always been one to take pictures, so I'm grateful for the many photo albums full of images as they were growing. I wish I'd written down more milestones though; ages when they learned a new skill or said certain words for the first time. Photographs can't always capture things like that.

Memories become rare treasures when death steals our ability to make new ones. Surrounding me with Tyger's belongings had been my way of ensuring I wouldn't forget anything. Packing some of it away was the right decision because the time had come. Besides, the most important reminders are carried in my heart and soul. They are a part of me; endless sources of joy and the occasional tear, as well.

Years continue to pass since Tyger crossed over and several significant objects remain here in the physical world. These are items with meaning which keep finding their way into my hands. This is all Tyger's doing, of course. I have no doubt of his involvement, even if the messengers are unaware.

As the second anniversary of his death approached, I was in a much better place emotionally than I had been the previous year. Rather than being weighed down by grief, my mood had lightened. My desire was to celebrate his life and not focus on his death. After all, it was also the date of his birth. He would've been fifty-nine if he were still on this side of the veil.

In addition to being Tyger's birthday/anniversary, July 30, 2016, was also my parents' wedding anniversary. The date marked fifty years of marriage for them which would've been cause for celebration if they were still in the physical realm. I intended to spend the day honoring the people who gave me life and the man who taught me how to live.

There is no right or wrong way to grieve. I give myself permission to go with whatever I'm feeling in any given moment. This time it was joy and I embraced it from the time I awoke that morning. It was a Saturday, so I had the day off. Sophia was with me... nothing new there. She's at my house just about every Friday to Sunday for our grandma/granddaughter time.

We awoke early and ate breakfast, then packed our things for the beach. Weather permitting, we were there every weekend. The forecast called for sunny skies and highs in the eighties, so it was "all systems go." I imagined how happy it made Tyger seeing us sticking to our routine, despite the date on the calendar. The last thing he would ever want is for Sophia to miss out on something she loved, just so I could sit around feeling sad all day. No chance of that happening; I was as eager to get my toes in the sand as she was.

We always left early to beat the rush of traffic. Saturday is a big beach day in New England, so it was best to head out in the morning. Once there, I set up our things with Sophia impatiently waiting for me to apply her sunscreen so she could dash off to check the water temperature. Soon, she was back, ready to begin a construction project with her pails and shovels of various sizes.

I stretched out on my lounger, drawing a deep breath of the sea air. "Ahh, this is what it's all about," I thought as I smiled thinking of my parents, Tyger, and the significance of the day. It was great feeling happy to be alive.

Sophia was digging away, I assumed on her latest version of a castle. After a short while, she said, "Look, Nani, I made you a surprise."

I raised my sunglasses to see her creation and instead of mounds of wet sand, there was a large, perfectly shaped heart just past the foot of my chair. Hearts have always been a big sign from Tyger; he most often sends them through Sophia, but it had been a while since he communicated in this way. I acknowledged his expression of joy that his girls were doing what they love.

Sophia and I decided to walk along the shore to the shallow marsh area. As we made our way to the far end, the sand was wet where the water had receded a short time before. Sophia noticed snails near the water's edge and called me over to see them. I looked down and spotted a heart traced in the sand with the letters "I, L, Y" etched inside. An acronym for "I love you." This was an obvious message from Tyger. Someone who'd been there previously had left this inscription, but Tyger led us to the location in order to make his presence felt.

We enjoyed our beach time and arrived home around three o'clock. My son, Aaron, came in from work shortly after and was barely through the door when Sophia asked, "Daddy, can we go to the park?"

Despite our having spent hours in the sun, Sophia insisted on another outing. She loves being outside and never overlooks an opportunity for more.

I said to her, "Soph, it's Mike's birthday. Do you want to go with Nani to the cemetery?" She answered, "No, I want to go with Daddy to the park."

Aaron said yes, and the two of them were off.

It may seem strange to some, but Sophia is often the one who suggests we go to the cemetery to visit "Mikey's grave." They shared—and still share—an incredible bond and she seldom turns down a chance to visit. Her reaction and joy at the thought of going to the park was right in line with my pleasant feelings. Neither of us was sad and I knew how happy Tyger was about that.

The weather was beautiful, so I decided to wear a sundress for my visit. It was his birthday and I wanted to look nice. Who cared if I was going to his burial site? I wore something that reflected my desire to celebrate the man I love and it felt right.

Earlier in the week, I'd spoken with friends of Tyger's and mine. They wanted to meet me at his plot and said they had something for me. I arrived with flowers and balloons to lay at the site. Our friends pulled up behind me and we exchanged hugs. They are a married couple, Duane and Donna, nicknamed "Duke." Duane and Tyger had formed a close friendship in our years working together at a local casino and I knew Duane, as well. Tyger was a frequent visitor at their home and the four of us had hopes of spending lots of couple's time together. Unfortunately, Tyger's sudden passing had put an end to those plans.

In his years as a cook in the main kitchen of the casino, Tyger was in charge of the large rotary or deck ovens. Duane is in the Engineering department and when he heard they planned to dismantle the oven and do some remodeling, he wondered if anything from "Big Mike's oven" could be saved. The only salvageable piece was the door handle. It was made of wood, the one part of the unit that wasn't stainless steel. Duane thought about the countless times Tyger had opened and closed the door and how much of him was embedded in this object, which was soon to be discarded. Duane was granted permission to keep the handle and he wanted me to have it.

We were standing near Tyger's headstone as they shared this incredible story. As I took the heirloom from Duane, I felt a surge of energy.

In tears, Duke asked, "Isn't it beautiful? Smell it, I think it smells like Mike. Maybe you can have it carved into something. It's yours now, to keep."

I was overwhelmed by the magnitude of the gesture. Not only had Duane thought to ask for this priceless treasure, he'd done so on my behalf. Somewhere deep in my soul, I had no doubt of Tyger's involvement. A little whisper, a tiny suggestion planted in Duane's mind; so subtle he hadn't even realized the thought came from someone else. He hadn't ignored it though; he acted on it and in doing so, made this unforgettable moment a reality. There is no possible way to repay this couple for such an amazing gift.

We spent quite a while talking and reminiscing. There was laughter and plenty of tears. Through it all, the lightness in my spirit remained as it had been the entire day. We exchanged more hugs before getting into our vehicles to go our separate ways. On my way home, I was lost in thought, still reeling from the enormity of what took place. Traffic was slowing down for a red light and as I glanced at the car up ahead, the license plate caught my eye. It wasn't the letters but the number sequence that I was struck by...111.

Oh, my goodness. There they were, right in front of me. The numbers Tyger had been using for months to get my attention. The number "eleven" which I'd come to understand was also a signal from the Universe that I'm on the right path, and to keep moving forward. A spiritual breadcrumb as plain as the nose on my face. Undeniable proof that love never dies and neither do we. A perfect way to cap off a day full of wonders.

I spoke out loud, "Thank you, baby. I love you and I feel you loving me. Always."

This sign from Tyger was an expression of his happiness for my joy. The instant I recognized his message, a powerful current flowed through my body; a sensation of protective warmth. I reached out to touch the picture of him which is mounted on the console. This is my reaction whenever I'm in the car and something occurs that connects us. I placed my right index and middle finger on the photo and hold them there for several seconds.

It's a symbolic way of making contact, but my attention is focused deeply on our love. My breathing becomes slow and deep and I detect a brief exchange of energy.

I interpret these events as a direct line of communication being opened between us. The small window of time spanning his reaching out and my acknowledgment opens a channel between us. The essence of our spirits meets in that tiny space and that's what I pick up on. A smile instantly spreads across my face and tears fill my eyes. There is no denying the power in these moments.

Tyger encourages me as I progress, just as he did in physical life. He understands the conflict I face trying to move forward while still holding on to what we shared. As I continue on my path, the goal is not to leave him behind, rather to incorporate the impression he's made in all I do. He's aware of the strength drawn from our bond and finds different ways of demonstrating this knowledge.

A few weeks before Christmas, I heard from Tyger's niece. She said she had something of his for me. Her exact words were, "This is so *him*, and I want you to have it." It took us a couple days to connect so I was in suspense, having no idea what it could be. She stopped by one evening after work, with a small item under her arm. As she handed it to me, I recognized the red, triangle-shaped box. It was Tyger's Charlie Brown Tree.

This had been the source of many laughs, years earlier when he'd told me about his "Charlie Brown Christmas Tree." I'd pictured an old, pitiful sight, like the one in the classic cartoon, propped up in a corner. It was quite a surprise when he revealed it was an actual replica of the tree used in the Peanuts cartoon special.

I was overjoyed to have such a wonderful memory in my possession. A perfect representation of Tyger's personality and his unique way of being simultaneously silly and sweet. I hugged his niece so tightly and thanked her for making the season that much brighter with this welcome addition to my holiday décor. As she was leaving I said, "I'm not touching it until Sophia comes this weekend. It will be her job to decorate it and find the perfect location."

When Sophia arrived, I showed her the box and explained this was Mike's tree. We removed it from the box and assembled the pieces. Her next words were so precious.

"Nani, I feel bad for Mike."

Puzzled by her statement, I asked, "Why Soph?"

She said, "Well, we have a big tree and all Mike had was this tiny one."

I explained, "No Soph, Mike *loved* this tree. This is just like the one in the Charlie Brown cartoon and that's why he bought it. He could've had a big one if he wanted, but he really liked this one because it's funny."

"Ohhh," she said, relieved that he hadn't been slighted in any way.

I had some miniature gold bulbs and red bows, so I handed them to her and she placed them on the branches. The finished product was beautiful and I laughed as I imagined Tyger thinking we'd overdone it. She'd done such a nice job and I could hear him saying, "You made it look too nice, it's supposed to be pathetic." It was a funny thought as I stood there smiling at this well-decorated twig, prominently displayed next to our "big tree," as Sophia referred to it. I had no doubt Tyger loved every minute of watching his girls at work. His little tree was right where it belonged. Of course, he knew that since it was his idea in the first place. He just needed his niece to make the delivery.

As I sit here, writing this chapter, Tyger continues to make his presence known. When I write, I always listen to soft jazz. It's a preference because of the mellow vibe and lack of distracting vocals. I had typed the first few words of the paragraph which describes Tyger's niece contacting me about something she wanted me to have. As I finished the line, "This is so *him*," the theme song to the Peanuts cartoon came on the music channel. I'm sure you remember Schroeder seated at the piano, playing that tune, titled, "Linus and Lucy." This actually happened and I jumped right out of my seat.

I could hardly believe my ears. I walked back and forth multiple times to the TV, returned to the computer, then across the room again. I read the song information, listed at the bottom left of the screen, *Linus and Lucy by Vince Guaraldi.* I turned to Tyger's picture on my bureau, half laughing and half crying, as I pointed at his face with my pencil, "You are something else. I mean, really… are you kidding me right now? I can't believe you. I hear you, but I can't believe the things you do. Wow, just wow!"

Now come on, who on earth would ever expect to hear that song in the middle of a smooth jazz rotation? I listen to this channel at least five nights a week and they repeat many selections. I don't ever recall this one being played before. What are the odds it would come on at the exact moment I'm about to write about his Charlie Brown tree? I need a mathematician to work out the probabilities on this one because they must be unfathomable. We know exactly why this happened. Tyger was letting me know in his grand way that he's right here, active, aware, and very much alive.

These are the absolute, light bulb above your head, smack you in the face, mind-blowing, events that prove what's available to all of us, if we listen with open hearts. A flaw in the human condition is the need to see, hear, taste, and touch everything in order to prove it's real. All we have to do is expand our consciousness beyond what we've been conditioned to believe, and the impossible suddenly becomes not only possible, but probable.

The memories Tyger and I made in our time on this earthly plane help to sustain me. He maintains our connection by having meaningful items delivered into my hands by others, which helps satisfy the physical aspect. Then, he'll send songs or number sequences to get my mental attention. In either case, these tangible reminders serve to reiterate our loved ones are not lost to us. I've already accepted that truth. What he's doing now, is helping to convince all of you. How's he doing so far?

Chapter Twelve
The Fact of the Matter

THERE ARE MANY REASONS why folks find it difficult to accept our status as eternal beings. From their perspective, the concept of us being powerful creators seems far-fetched and highly questionable. For some, it's based on a steadfast devotion to religious doctrine. Others prefer to stay within the confines of what mainstream society has deemed "normal." There are the scientific types who will only accept measurable processes and conclusive findings.

I am not a crusader, charging in to change the hearts and minds of the non-believers. The truth is only those in vibrational alignment to the message will be capable of receiving. I am a woman who has witnessed a remarkable transformation in her life, which began by being open to possibilities. As layer upon layer of proof was laid out before, within, and around me, my soul, or authentic self, stepped forward. My intent is to shine brightly and light the way for all who are ready to realize their potential.

In the early months of my grief, I found peace in reading. The subject of the afterlife resonated with me, specifically stories focused on near-death experiences. One such book, *Proof of Heaven* by Dr. Eben Alexander, was particularly intriguing. I read more than a dozen books on the topic, but this account differed from others because it was told by a man of science. Dr. Alexander was a neurosurgeon; trained to discount anything not proven by hard facts. There couldn't have seemed a more unlikely candidate for traveling beyond the veil, yet it happened and he returned with a need to share his extraordinary adventure with the world.

Dr. Alexander succumbed, without warning, to a rare illness which caused a shut-down of the area of the brain which controls thought and emotion. He remained in a coma for seven days while his physicians exhausted every possible treatment for his condition. During that period, he traveled with an angelic guide to another realm of pure love and peace. He tells of interacting with a Divine Source before returning to his body just as the medical team was on the brink of stopping their efforts to reverse his condition.

I would recommend this book to anyone who is looking for insight into what lies beyond physical life. The descriptions are vivid and thought provoking. I went on to read his second work, *Map of Heaven*, which discloses more on the subject. As fascinating as the story is, I found the unlikelihood of a scientific mind becoming a firm believer to be the most captivating part.

I was under the impression this blending of science and spirituality was a rare occurrence, but I was mistaken. There are many in the scientific community who are not only coming to accept the possibility of a higher consciousness, but are offering evidence of its existence. Studies have been taking place worldwide, involving the mapping of brainwaves and the effects of positive thinking on healing illnesses and much more. This is an extremely exciting time to be alive.

There are many on the cutting edge of this new frontier which is actually based on centuries old information. A friend introduced me to the work of one man who explains his research and findings in terms anyone can relate to and understand. Dr. Joe Dispenza travels the world, speaking and conducting seminars on improving life by changing the way we think and our emotional responses. A reprogramming of the brain, in essence.

Over two decades ago, this doctor was involved in a biking accident which crushed part of his spine. He was advised by several physicians to undergo surgical procedures in order to avoid paralysis. The risks of the operation involved living with a severe disability and life-long pain. He opted to look inward for answers and decided to turn down the surgery. Dr. Joe began focusing on healing by altering thought patterns and literally changing his mind. In what was considered a miraculous feat, the doctor was back to work in ten weeks, walking on his own, and pain-free. He goes into great detail in his book, *Evolve Your Brain*. Inspired by his experiences, this is a telling of the methods and practices which resulted in his new outlook on life.

Dr. Joe has a doctorate in chiropractic care; however, while an undergraduate, he studied neurology, neuroscience, brain function, chemical biology, and memory formation. As a researcher, his focus has been quantum physics which led to several amazing revelations about human potential and what lies beyond physical abilities. The remarkable events which took place following his accident prompted him to seek out individuals who, like himself, had been able to improve physiological conditions by retraining their minds.

Dr. Joe has conducted detailed studies on unexplained healing or spontaneous remissions which took place in people with chronic illnesses. They all seemed to have a common mindset. Each subject understood the impact of negative emotions and thought patterns on their health, and how this led to them becoming sick. By consciously addressing and adjusting their thinking, old behaviors were eliminated and conditions began to improve.

This theory was proven true in my own life after receiving the results of a routine mammogram. Each year, I go for my annual exam and the findings are normal. The process is always the same: After the test, the notice arrives in the mail from the Diagnostic Imaging Department of the hospital. I open it, see "normal," and life continues on for another year.

This time, I had no reason to think the results would be any different. When the letter came, I tore off the perforated edges, unfolded it, and quickly searched for the familiar word. This time it wasn't there. In its place, the first line read, "Your recent mammography examination showed a finding that requires additional imaging studies for a complete evaluation. Most such findings are benign (not cancer)."

At another stage in my life, this statement would've been cause for alarm. Had I received such a thing prior to learning of the damaging effects of fear and worry, I'm sure my reaction would have been apprehension. Visions of the worst case scenario would have, more than likely, flooded my imagination.

There was none of that. My first thought was, "I'll go for the test but there's nothing wrong with me." Not only did I tell myself this, I believed every word. It wasn't spoken in defiance or in some attempt to trick my brain into acceptance. I said what I meant and meant what I said. That was the end of it.

The following day, I received a call from my primary care doctor letting me know they had ordered the additional imaging. I listened calmly, making note of the appointment date and time. After adding it to the calendar on my phone, I returned to business as usual. There was no need to dwell on it or even share the news with anyone else. I simply refused to feed any energy into it, whatsoever.

My focus remained right where it had been before receiving the results. I was busy promoting my book, actively seeking venues to speak, writing blog posts, and living my life. There was no way I'd put any of that on hold in order to follow the old habits of worrying myself sick. That phrase is a literal description of what worry does to our physical state, by the way. It's the equivalent of calling up everything we don't want to happen which is why I refuse to entertain such thoughts.

When the day arrived for my appointment, I was my usual self. There was no tightness in my chest area or butterflies in my stomach. My mind was already past the events taking place as I pondered the subject of my next blog post. I listened as the technician explained the details of the mammogram and the ultrasound to follow. She said the radiologist would speak to me immediately upon completion, so there'd be no waiting for results. I'd leave that day with answers.

I talked and laughed through both procedures, then waited for the doctor to come in and explain. She entered the room and extended her hand.

"Hello, Diane. I'm Dr. Spellman. I have some good news for you. The calcifications we saw on the original images are just the way I'd like them to look. The spacing is good with no dense areas and that's what we want. I'll have you come back in six months to repeat the detailed imaging, and then we'll get you back on your annual schedule. Do you have any questions for me?"

I smiled and said, "Nope. You said exactly what I knew you would say."

She returned the smile as she answered, "I'm glad to know that."

During the ultrasound, prior to speaking with the doctor, my mind drifted back to those early weeks and months after Tyger passed. Back then, I prayed for my life to end. Each time the slightest twinge passed through my body, I would say, "Oh good, maybe I have cancer and I'll die soon."

Sounds awful, right?

I know it does, but I couldn't stand the agony of being here without him. I had directed a fair amount of energy toward my desire to leave this physical world. Was it possible those thoughts were now manifesting and something would be found?

Even as I pondered the possibility, there was no fear. My mind had been made up so regardless of what the results showed, illness was not an option for me. After the doctor shared her good news, there was no sigh of relief because I was already sure of what I'd hear.

Having this personal example to refer to validates the theories and findings in current research. I accept responsibility for my physical condition and understand the key role my thoughts play in my well-being.

In the classes and seminars held by Dr. Joe, he explains the process thoroughly. The practice of reliving our current reality develops into a repetitive pattern of thought. This creates a state of being which, over time, becomes like a subconscious computer program, running on repeat. Memorized behaviors, emotional responses, beliefs, and perceptions fuel these patterns and keep us trapped. In other words, we become prisoners of our reactions to past experiences.

Adjusting the way we think causes us to feel differently, signaling genes that were once dormant. Chemical reactions within the body join forces with neurons in the brain and this remission, or healing is set in motion. This is the evolutionary process of breaking the habit of being ourselves.

Reading his articles and hearing him speak in recorded events, I found the logic impressive. So many express a desire to change or improve conditions, yet so few are actually willing to make adjustments. When you think about it, isn't it pretty ridiculous to keep feeling, saying, and doing the same things over and over and expecting different results? It makes perfect sense that a desire for a new outcome must begin with a fresh approach to thought patterns.

As I studied the teachings of Dr. Joe and others like him, I had a scientific explanation for the first time of how I've been able to survive the horrific event of Tyger's passing and the grief that followed. It was accomplished by holding tight to gratitude (an elevated emotion) and my dedication to loving myself. I had no idea I was actually altering my chemical composition by doing this. All I knew was it felt better to show appreciation for our love and "do Diane" than it did to focus on what was lost and remain immersed in sadness.

Tyger's passion introduced a sense of empowerment into my life which caused me to stop living in a reactive state to past events. My willingness to enjoy the moment and anticipate a bright future was sparked by our union and death had not been able to rob me of this. I am determined to honor the man I love by living life to the fullest. It began with a choice and blossomed into an enhancement of mind, body, and soul.

As the creator of my own reality, I consciously avoid directing my energy toward anything that leads to unhappiness. Combining clear intent with positive emotion is guiding me toward a new state of being. Gratitude is expressed for the expectation of abundance I see flowing into my life. The neurological response to this vision, which occurs in the frontal lobe, is the same whether or not it has yet to manifest in the physical. Live imaging of this area of the brain has proven the wave activity is identical, whether something is viewed through our sense of vision or via the mind's eye.

Think about that for a moment...

The reaction in this active nerve center is exactly the same regardless of physically possessing our desires or by simply *believing* we have them. This is one of many astonishing discoveries made in the field of neuroscience which continues to advance. I don't know about you, but to me, that sounds an awful lot like creating reality.

The vast majority of us have barely begun to realize our potential. As I learn more about the inner workings of the brain, it motivates me to continue exploring and developing. I am eager to break old habits and continuously reinvent myself. The person I am today is far more enlightened than who I was five years ago and my goal is to keep expanding. I mentioned in an earlier chapter how easy it is for me to accept what's logical. My retention rate is high with anything that makes good sense. Reading conclusive findings which support spiritual views and Universal Law is both encouraging and exciting.

For me, the ultimate achievement would be fine tuning my awareness to the point of no longer submitting to situations with familiar emotions. I'm not there yet, but I catch myself much sooner when I slip into those old ways. Recognition is the first step to addressing the behavior so I'm moving in the right direction.

When events come up in our lives, we get caught up in our reaction to it which ends up staying with us long after the occurrence has passed. There is a tendency amongst us humans to drag things out much farther than we should and I've certainly been guilty of this in the past. A friend shared a quotation which applies here:

"Was it a bad day or a bad five minutes that you milked all day?"

I'm becoming conscious of my usual responses to the unexpected, which over time, have become a habit. This awareness activates a new experience in my brain and neurons automatically fire in different patterns, creating connections that weren't there previously. You could say a new version of me is launched in that moment.

I am highly selective in my choice of words. We tend to talk ourselves into things by making statements that bring about adverse effects. Take a case of the sniffles, for example. There was a time when my reaction to that would've been, "I'm getting sick" or "I don't feel well." Since gaining this understanding of the power we possess, I divert my attention away from the physical symptoms. My response to comments about my condition is, "I feel fine." As you can imagine, this raises an eyebrow or two but the response of others isn't my concern. What matters most is my belief that all is well. Anything less is detrimental to my health.

My awareness has grown to the point where I recognize when others are perpetuating any sort of affliction. I nearly cringe when I hear someone say, "No matter what I do, it doesn't make me feel any better" or "I can't get rid of this." We have been conditioned for so long to focus on how things are rather than how we'd like them to be. This is a difficult tendency to break but essential to our health and quality of life. Simply put, we have far more control of our current situations than we've ever given ourselves credit for.

The connection I share with Tyger across time and space is all the proof I'll ever need of how powerful we actually are. Having said that, I couldn't be happier to have my beliefs justified through analytical testing. The findings are closing the gap between views which were once in strong opposition to each other. My enthusiasm is a result of this middle ground and the dialogue which includes similar language from both sides.

The word, "mind" is defined by the field of science as "the brain at work." I'm fascinated by this configuration of neurons and gray matter, set in motion. Its capabilities support the concepts of the Law of Attraction. Solid explanations are being offered for our ability to transform ourselves from one state of being to another. As studies progress, evidence is surfacing for those who have difficulty accepting esoteric concepts.

At first glance, the blending of spirituality with scientific fact seems impossible, but appearances can be deceiving. In the very least, this union prompts us to ask more questions. The quest for answers is the driving force of the creative process. As research continues, I have no doubt it will result in a clearer understanding and wider acceptance of our abilities. The facts are being compiled at an astonishing rate. For the receptive mind, the possibilities are endless, as infinite as life itself.

Before one can arrive at acceptance, the mind must be open. Wondrous things are available to those willing to receive.

Listen...did you hear that?

Chapter Thirteen
Whispers From Within

AS I PROGRESS in the awakening process, I find myself increasingly tuned into the little voice inside. It's often referred to as intuition or having a feeling about something. There are times it presents itself as a nagging thought that refuses to be ignored. I've come to accept these occurrences as nudges from the spirit realm.

In some cases, our loved ones on the other side are offering guidance. They have the ability to see tomorrow much clearer than we can see today. With this panoramic vision, they prompt us with suggestions or offer direction when we've strayed from our paths. This isn't done in a forceful way and we always have the final say, since we possess free will. In my experience, I fare much better when I heed those thoughts that appear out of nowhere.

This was the case, just before Christmas. My holiday spirit was going strong and I was eagerly anticipating the celebration. The same joy I'd felt at Thanksgiving was with me as I wrapped gifts for my sons and granddaughter.

We planned to have our family dinner and open presents on Christmas Eve since Sophia had to go home that night in order to be with her mom in the morning. Santa was coming to their house so she had to be there to leave him cookies and milk, and of course, carrots for his reindeer.

Since there wouldn't be any little ones around to get me up early on December 25th, my goal was to spend the day relaxing on the couch, watching movies. One of those rare times I'd stay in my PJ's and be lazy. Tyger's family was getting together and I was more than welcome to join them, but my mind was set on doing nothing and enjoying it. Two days before the holiday, I began feeling like I should go. There was a battle taking place in my mind, one side arguing the case for lounging in the house and the opposing team pushing me to stop by and see everyone.

As the scales started tipping in favor of going, another thought came of bringing something of Tyger's as a gift for his dad. Tyger's father was born on Christmas day, and this year he would be ninety-one. I was overcome with a need to give him something that had belonged to his son. That wasn't a problem since I have so many of his belongings, but what should I bring?

After a while, I remembered I had Tyger's bible in the drawer of my nightstand. He'd written his name and the year on the inside cover, "Michael T. Johnson, 1997." This would be a wonderful keepsake for his Dad; it had been important to Tyger and contained his handwriting. Instantly I felt this was the right thing to do.

I followed through on the idea, which seemed to come out of the blue, and Mr. Johnson was so appreciative. As I handed him the box, I said, "This is for you, Dad. It was Tyger's and I want you to have it." He looked up at me from his comfortable chair and said, "Thank you so much. That was so thoughtful of you. Are you sure my heart can take it? I got a weak heart, you know." I laughed and said, "Oh no you don't, you have the strongest heart in the room."

He was touched by the gesture, especially when I pointed out his son's signature inside. There was no doubt I'd made a good choice by getting dressed and showing up. It was obvious to me, who'd set his plan in motion. Tyger knew it would not only benefit his father, but me, as well. The few hours spent with his family were filled with laughter and love.

Christmas had been wonderful. Dinner and gifts with Aaron, Markie, and Sophia the night before, then time spent with family at the home of my cousins, Angy and Dewayne. They host Christmas Eve every year and we had a great time, as always. The following day, after leaving Tyger's family, I came home and watched movies while enjoying some "holiday cheer" in the form of eggnog and rum. I was filled with gratitude for my festive spirit and positive mindset.

When I returned to work after the holiday break, a girl in the office asked how the book was doing.

"Really well," I answered. "Sales are steady and readers continue to share how much our story is helping them. The reactions are pretty emotional."

"That's great," she responded. "Have you thought about contacting any holistic fairs and asking to be a vendor? My mom goes all the time and bought a few books at the last one."

It was like a light bulb suddenly appeared above my head, and I said, "I would love to get involved with something like that, but I don't have any contacts in the community."

"I'm sure I can get a few names for you," she said. "In the meantime, just Google 'holistic fairs' and see what comes up."

What a fantastic suggestion! Patrons of this type of event were the perfect audience for our story. We'd already had much success in the mainstream, so I could only imagine how it would be to connect with those whose beliefs are a match to my own. As many times as I'd turned to the Internet in the past, why hadn't it occurred to me to try this? Oh well, no sense wasting time kicking myself. It was a wonderful idea and I couldn't wait to get home and begin searching.

I settled into my usual spot on the sofa and powered up the laptop. In the search box, I typed "Holistic Fairs Connecticut" and in a few seconds, there were several listings to choose from. The first one I selected sounded like a good fit. The full calendar for 2017 hadn't been released yet, but there was an event coming up in less than three months. It was in another part of the state, less than an hour's drive. I located the contact information for the organizer and logged into my personal email account to express my interest.

I began composing my note when a quiet thought entered my mind. "Maybe I should send this from the address linked to my website instead." As though I were answering the idea, my silent response was, "No, this one is fine." Immediately, I felt another urge to switch accounts and this time I complied. I hadn't checked that inbox in a while since it doesn't see much activity. I wondered if anything new had arrived, as I waited the few seconds it took to sign on.

There was one message waiting for me and it was from my dear friend, Lee. I was pleasantly surprised to hear from her. In the opening, she wished my family and me a Merry Christmas and my reaction was, "how nice of her to think of us for the holidays."

She continued on, and I became increasingly intrigued by each word.

"I wanted to pass some information along to you. My friend shared this request for a few new faces to speak at a local spiritualist church during 2017. They meet the second and fourth Sunday of the month and will pay for your time. A brief, fifteen-minute talk on a spiritual subject is ideal."

"I had a conversation with the woman who runs the program because I was curious to hear specifically what she was doing and the topics she was interested in, etc. We talked for quite a bit (she's a medium so it went in that direction.) Anyway, long story short, I mentioned you and Big Mike and she said, matter-of-factly actually, "THIS" story would be a great topic. So, I'm passing it on to you. She has the following dates in 2017 available if you have an interest to add them to your book tour: August 13, September 10, November 12, and December 10.

Love and Light, Lee"

My initial reaction to what she'd said, was shock. Had I read that correctly? Were they looking for speakers and willing to pay? This wasn't only a chance to share our story, but another a milestone in my journey. I clicked "reply" to thank Lee for thinking of me and when the screen to compose a message appeared, I recalled why I'd logged on.

It had to be Tyger telling me to use this account because he knew I'd find this information from Lee. If I hadn't listened, who knows how long it would've been before I even knew it was there and could've missed out on the opportunity.

My intent was to contact the person holding the holistic fair, and now, in addition to that, I'd be receiving even more exposure. Rather than one event, it had become two with the potential for more. All of it made possible by simply heeding a gentle whisper in my mind. Something that could've been easily ignored, turned into a new connection between souls. No matter how many times this guidance comes to me, my reaction is amazement. I am in awe of the workings of the Universe and what's available if we stay open.

The vastness of who we are is so expansive it's difficult to comprehend in this human form. Many are quick to dismiss things like this but for those who have tapped into a higher consciousness, there is meaning in every instance. We have a divine support team made up of loved ones who have gone on before us. They don't float away into the hereafter, not by a long shot. Our well-being is important to them and help is available to those willing to accept.

My goddaughter, Crystal, is one of a handful of family members who speaks the same "spiritual language" as I do. She has delivered messages to me from Tyger and we've had many deep conversations on the topic of our authentic selves and the power we possess. We are extremely close, although geographically, we live quite a distance from each other. When I received the news that her grandmother had passed suddenly, my heart instantly hurt for her pain.

She believes wholeheartedly there is no end to us; only a shedding of the physical form. Regardless of this knowledge, I was all too aware of the sting of grief, especially when death came without warning. Acceptance of our eternal status is not a cure-all for pain so I needed to connect with her.

When Crystal answered the phone, I noticed the strength in her voice. I was relieved she seemed to be doing well, but struggled with holding back my own tears at the thought of all she'd been through in the preceding hours. She told me there had been some rough moments, but the overall feeling was a sense of calm. Crystal knew her grandmother was tired of fighting to be here and found peace as she crossed over.

During our conversation, I reminded Crystal to stay open to any communications from beyond the veil. It was important to stay mindful and notice the little things we sometimes miss; lyrics to a song, number sequences, thoughts that appear out of nowhere, electronic devices behaving erratically; anything that caused her to pause and question its origin was most likely her grandmother trying to get her attention. Of course, she was already aware of this since she believes so strongly.

I would reach out via text periodically over the following days, but didn't want to bombard my goddaughter with calls. Sometimes the bereaved need space; time to process what's happened and absorb the changes in routine and life in general.

On New Year's Eve, I considered giving her a quick ring, but decided against it. She has the support of her husband and son, so I knew she'd contact me, if needed.

While many attend parties to celebrate this special night, my days of doing that were long since over. Sophia and I baked cupcakes early in the evening, and then after she went to bed, I made myself comfortable in front of the TV with some cheese and crackers and a nice glass of white zinfandel. It would be me and "Dick Clark's Rockin' New Year's Eve" until the ball dropped at midnight, and I was perfectly fine with the plan.

In the final seconds of 2016, as the countdown commenced, my emotional state was excitement. This was the first time since Tyger's passing that ringing in a new year filled me with joy. I sat on the edge of the couch, counting out loud, "five, four, three, two, one...Happy New Year!" I shouted and clapped, undeterred by the fact that I was alone in the room.

Springing from my seat, I stood close to the large portrait of Tyger, hanging on the living room wall. It was located where I could see it clearly from my usual spot, but I needed to be up close and personal. I looked at his smiling face and spoke, "Happy New Year, baby. This past year was incredible. Our book came out and is helping so many people. 2017 will take us farther than I've ever imagined. I have never been so sure of anything in my entire life. Thank you so much for loving me; for coming into my life and giving me the tools I needed to not only survive, but thrive. I am so grateful and I love you."

I brought my right hand to my lips, kissed the first three fingers, and pressed them against his lips. Even though it was the glass of the frame I made contact with, this gesture was more than symbolic. I sensed a real connection, an exchange of energy and the warmth of his approval. I couldn't help but think how far I'd come from years past when tears fell and sadness overwhelmed me. I acknowledged the difference and embraced the anticipation of abundance and success flowing into my life experience. With dry eyes and a grateful heart, I was on cloud nine.

My thoughts turned to Crystal and I wondered how she was feeling. Rather than risk waking her with a call, I thought to send a text. Nothing too jovial; a simple "I love you" was all I planned to say. As I spelled out the words, other sentiments came to mind. I decided to go on typing, "I love you and promise your aching heart will heal. A new year has arrived with infinite possibilities. Your grandma will continue to show how close she is. Great big hugs to you."

I gave it a quick proofread before pressing "send." For several seconds, the message didn't go anywhere. Soon, I received a notice from my carrier, "Unable to send message." I selected "retry send" once, but the same response arrived a short time later. "This is so strange," I thought to myself. "The few times this happened before, they always go through on the second try."

It was getting late, so I went to bed. Sophia was spread out on my mattress sound asleep, so I moved her over and got under the covers. Hopefully, at some point, the message would be delivered so Crystal would know I'd been thinking of her. About two hours later, I was awakened by the notification sound on my phone. It was Crystal, letting me know she'd received my message multiple times.

She wrote, "Grandma is not playing. That text just came through like eight times."

I smiled as I set the device back on the nightstand and drifted off to sleep.

In the morning, Crystal called to explain further. Apparently, the communication had arrived in two parts. The first half, which came through repeatedly, said, "I love you and promise your aching heart will heal. A new year has arrived with infinite possibilities. Your grandma will continue to show how close she is" and that was it. A short time later, multiple copies of the following arrived, "Great big hugs to you."

The joy in Crystal's voice was unmistakable as she described how important it must have been to her grandmother that those words be received. I shared in her happiness because I know how wonderful it is to hear from those we love on the other side. The best part was, I was now being used as the communication tool. It feels just as great being the deliverer as it does as the receiver.

There was more to it, as Crystal went on to share. Her husband, Donald, suggested they take an early morning walk on the beach before her shift at work. As they strolled along, a man was passing and remarked that one of the crab traps seemed to be stuck. Donald helped him reset it and they wished one another a happy new near. As the trio was about to part ways, the man turned to them and said, "What am I doing? I'm French and we hug." He embraced each of them tightly, wished them well and continued on in the opposite direction. Crystal and Donald looked at each other as they realized Grandma had managed to give them a "great big hug."

There are so many behind-the-scenes components to this. On the surface, some would say it was a glitch in the system that caused the message to be delivered as it was. This may have been a technological malfunction but it came as a result of manipulation with a purpose. As a direct result, the connection between Crystal and her grandmother was emphasized. The repeated reference to "great big hugs" was driven home when this stranger offered one to both of them, almost as an afterthought. The man got the hint and acted on it.

Donald suggesting they go for an early morning walk, also happened by design. They had to be in that exact place in order to encounter this stranger who had an important component of the communication. He added the physical aspect in the embrace between them. As you consider everything that took place in the culmination of these events, it's nearly impossible not to be awestruck by the workings of the spirit realm.

Sophia and I got up and made our usual breakfast, pancakes and scrambled eggs. As we sat eating, she casually began to speak "Nani, you should be a Life Coach. When people die and their families don't know what to do, they can call on the phone and talk to you. Or, they can talk to you in person, you know, like Life Coaches do."

Now, bear in mind, this is a seven-year-old child saying this. I'm used to my granddaughter coming out with unexpected things, but this was a stretch, even for her. My mind sprang into action. Wondering how in the world she knew anything about life coaches or what they do, I calmly answered, "Yes Soph, I think you're right. That would be a good job for me."

I'm careful of how I respond when she makes these profound statements. I never want her to feel as though she's said anything wrong or strange. My outward appearance was normal but my thoughts were racing. "That remark was way too deep for someone her age. Where did she even hear the term, 'Life Coach'? It had to be Tyger, whispering into her thoughts. There's no other explanation"

This was followed by the usual rush that comes with the realization of contact from the other side. I waited a good hour or so, before bringing up the subject again. As I was brushing her hair, it seemed a good time to ask more questions.

"Soph, what makes you think Nani should be a life coach?" "Well" she began, "When Mike died you learned how it feels when someone you love dies. He taught you how to feel about that. Your supposed to help other people and teach them about their feelings when someone dies. That's what you're supposed to do, help them understand."

I concealed my heart-pounding reaction to her words with a short response, "You did a good job of explaining that Soph. Nani did learn a lot when Mike died and that's why I wrote my book. Thank you for sharing that with me. I love to help people." Her reply was a brief, "Mhmm" as she played with two Barbie dolls that were on the coffee table in front of her. She was oblivious to the depth of the subject matter and undisturbed by any of it. Life continued on as usual, in her world of innocence and love.

The year had begun with undeniable confirmation of the connection between worlds. 2016 ended on a high note and 2017 made an entrance just as grand. Sophia's revelation was a huge stamp of approval from the Universe; an encouragement to continue on my path and answer the calling of my soul. By seeking new venues to reach a broader audience I was actively advancing toward my goal and now I had proof of my alignment with a divine plan.

Paying attention to random thoughts and ideas is a must. Those subtle nuances are often meant to move us closer to where we belong. Thinking back, I can recall making numerous decisions I'd later come to regret. On almost every occasion, my reaction was, "I should've listened to that little voice." The reference was to the warning that had fleetingly come to mind before I chose to ignore it.

We've all used the phrase, "against my better judgment." The statement points to a subconscious awareness of the best route to take. These whispers originate in a place of knowing; well beyond human comprehension. It would serve us well to trust that inner voice. Whether it's coming from our higher selves or a loved one, neither would ever steer us wrong.

Chapter Fourteen
Intentional Diversion

ENERGY FLOWS WHERE ATTENTION GOES. This phrase is perhaps the most significant component of the law of attraction. The situation you find yourself in today is a direct result of what you've focused on in the days, weeks, months, or more, leading up to this moment. There is a tendency to look outside ourselves for someone or something to blame for our circumstances, especially if unpleasant. Truth is, it's an inside job.

My acceptance of the validity of this concept did not originate from reading it in a book or seeing it in a movie. I've observed the process at work in my own life. Acknowledging all the good things opens the door to receiving more. We fail ourselves by giving more attention to the lack of something than we do to the abundance of what we already have. Because our thoughts regulate our vibration, the Universe responds to what we focus on. It's a matter of aligning thought with desire.

I've become mindful of word usage. In Universal language, "yes" and "no" have the same meaning. Spend all day saying, "Yes, I am prosperous and I accept the abundance continuously flowing into my life," and the Universe responds by delivering more prosperity. The same rules apply when thinking, "No, I do not want to struggle with finances and go deeper into debt." By directing energy toward lack and hardship, we attract more financial problems and greater debt.

Do you recognize the difference in those statements?

I can't think of a better reason for keeping my thoughts positive.

Having gone through the harshness of grief, my daily goal is to live stress and worry-free. This has been relatively easy to accomplish by simply refusing to entertain drama. My ability to do this was put to the test during the 2016 Presidential campaign and election.

I've never been one to engage in political discussions or feel overly impassioned by any candidate. I'm no expert on the workings of government, but I know enough about the system of checks and balances to understand the President doesn't wield unlimited power. For me, it's more a matter of moral character. Not a single one of us is perfect. Everyone, including me, has things in their past they're not proud of. My decision of who to vote for is based on values I feel would best represent our nation, as a whole.

As the campaign ramped up, I found the comments and behavior of Donald Trump becoming more offensive. The energy being generated felt toxic, as though he were running on a platform of hate. He seemed to be preying on fear and pushing toward widening divides that already existed. I rarely watch news reports, but what I did see appeared too bizarre to be true. There was no way anyone with even an ounce of compassion could ever feel he was the right person to represent the United States. I'd later come to realize how mistaken I was.

Many of my friends on Facebook were sharing their political views. I did my best to refrain from doing the same. Other than the occasional "like" for something I agreed with, I steered clear of the subject. There is power in collective thought and countless elections have been won by candidates who were assisted by those who oppose their views. Remember, there is no differentiating between energy directed toward what's desired and what isn't. The multitudes protesting against Trump were fueling the same flow as his supporters. I didn't want any part of that, so I avoided making comments.

Each time I caught myself thinking about how much I disagreed with something he said or did, I shifted my focus to the flip side. This aligned my thoughts with what appealed to me and sent the current in the right direction. Unfortunately, many don't realize the damaging effects of protesting. The clearest path to victory is made by proclaiming our wants and supporting what we agree with.

Several great leaders in history had an understanding of this. Mother Teresa refused to attend a single anti-war rally, but stated she would gladly join in a gathering for world peace. Clearly, she understood how important it is to view things from a positive perspective. Rather than directing energy toward the atrocities of war and lowering the collective vibration, she was aware of the power and effect of focusing on love. Reverend Martin Luther King, Jr., also believed in taking a peaceful approach, as he fought tirelessly for civil rights and equality.

As the election results came in, I began to realize there was an actual possibility he could win. Up until that point, I'd been convinced it simply couldn't happen. However, I watched in disbelief as the tide shifted in his favor. When I awakened the following morning, I turned to CNN to receive the official news. It was true, Donald Trump had been elected as the forty-fifth President of these United States.

My reaction was disappointment. I was completely discouraged by the actions of some of my fellow Americans. Later that morning, I shared my thoughts in a Facebook post, "As I open my eyes on this new day, I am utterly embarrassed to be an American and my reaction to the results of the Presidential election is disgust. That being said, I will continue to live a life based on positivity and gratitude. This will not distract me from my purpose. God bless America."

It was an unexpected blow. Despite being enlightened in many ways, I am still living in this limited human form. As such, it can be difficult to strip away the layers of conditioning which have governed my thought processes and reactions for decades. The idea of Trump winning hadn't been something I considered possible. While I tried to remain unaffected, hearing the results felt like a punch to the midsection. The light of the world seemed diminished and I was having trouble tapping into my reserve of natural joy.

On the drive to work, I took note of the unfamiliarity in the air. Similar to my feelings following the tragic events of 9/11, there was a level of uncertainty. I was overcome by the sense that what I'd been sure of the day before, no longer existed.

"Who are these people that believe he's the right man for the job? Do I live and work next to them? Are they in line with me at the grocery store?"

These questions swirled in my mind all morning at my desk. Other than expressing disbelief over the election results, I said little to my coworkers. I was quietly reflecting and trying to tune out the TV in the waiting room. The major networks had interrupted regular programming so they were reporting his victory nonstop.

Shortly before lunchtime, I noticed a missed call from a family member. It wasn't someone I spoke with often, so I wondered what she might have wanted. Telling myself I'd ring her back on my break, I was about to put the phone down when a text came through from Angy, "Call me ASAP. Important." It was one of those messages that cause your heart to sink and stomach to flip upside-down. I slipped away to contact her and my suspicions were correct: it wasn't good news. She informed me our uncle had passed away and the family was gathering at the hospital.

I apologized to my boss, but told her I needed the rest of the day off. I had to be with my aunt and cousins the same way they'd rallied around me after Tyger's sudden passing. In my large family, the relationships cousins share is comparable to a bond between siblings. The afternoon was filled with tears, hugs, prayers, and love. Regardless of our age, losing a parent is not something any child wants to face. Having lost both of mine years earlier, I could relate to their sorrow.

Despite my knowledge of what lies beyond this stage of life, the pain of having to continue on without the physical presence of a loved one is undeniable. I took part in mourning the loss of a man who'd made a huge impact on our lives. There was plenty of sadness in the room but even more powerful was the love connecting us. Permeating the atmosphere, it was felt in every embrace, kind gesture and even the silent compassion of eyes meeting across a room.

At home, later that evening, it occurred to me the earlier distress regarding the presidency was gone. The angst had disappeared and been replaced with a new understanding. What matters most is the people I love, including myself. The time spent with family had shifted everything into proper perspective. Witnessing their heartache called attention to how insignificant the winner of the election is to my personal life experience. I have authority over my state-of-mind, but had temporarily lost sight of the fact. The sadness of my uncle's passing served as a course correction and a reminder to walk in love.

The point was driven home the following day when I was awakened by an early call. For a few seconds, I considered not answering, then decided to pick up. It was a dear friend, who proceeded to tell me her mother passed away. She was on her way to the hospital to say a final goodbye, and as you can imagine, extremely distraught. Ten minutes later, I was dressed and in the car, on my way to meet her so she wouldn't be alone. We sat together for most of the morning, alternating between tears and periods of silence. Words provide little comfort to the grieving heart but the company of a supportive friend does help.

Within a twenty-four hour period, two individuals I'd known my entire life had reached the end of their physical journeys. I watched two families I love suffer through this agony and I mourned along with them. As I marveled at the legacy left behind by these amazing souls, I gained a deeper understanding of what is deserving of my attention and what is not.

I may not be able to change the results of the election, but there is much I can do. I'm committed to evolving into a higher version of myself. I have the power to raise my vibration through self-love and gratitude. I'm capable of touching whoever I encounter with positive words and encouragement. I can offer inspiration through my writing and live speaking events. In the process, I'll continue to attract more of the same into my life experience. This generates a cycle of abundance which constantly replenishes itself. In other words, the more I give, the more I'll have available to share with others.

The secret of success has nothing to do with who makes the most noise or has the greatest weapons. The answer has always been and will forever be... love. My goal is to pour so much love into myself that it overflows into the lives of others and sets an example for my children and grandchildren to follow. Instead of discussing problems, I'll speak of solutions. Rather than fight against injustice, I will lend my support to causes I believe in.

As creators, each of us has the ability to transform the world. At some point, we're all faced with circumstances beyond our control. I've discovered it's best to turn my attention toward what can be regulated: emotions. They are conductors of energy and by exercising our ability to direct the flow, we go from helpless to limitless. That's the route to becoming the change we're seeking.

Chapter Fifteen
New Considerations

I'VE NEVER BEEN OVERLY FOND of change. Repetitive routines and behaviors have always been synonymous with security, in my mind. It wasn't until the devastating effects of Tyger's death and the grief that followed, that I dared to step cautiously out of my comfort zone.

I'm conservative by nature which is reflected in my clothing, make-up, hair style, tone of voice, and everything else, right down to the car I drive. I've been referred to as "straight-laced" and I'm about as by-the-book as they come. In my eyes, rules were made to be followed and not broken, so I'll never be the one you'd catch overstepping her bounds.

That's not to say I don't know how to enjoy myself. I love to dance and have a good time. I know how to have fun, but I'm certainly not the girl "shaking her groove thing" on a table top. I'm more apt to be away from the spotlight, quietly sipping my drink, then running to the dance floor with her girlfriends when they hear their favorite song. Classify me as far from boring, but nowhere near the life of the party either. I fall someplace in the middle.

Before meeting Tyger, I lived above a safety net. It was a place of comfort where I could maintain the status quo. Tyger shook things up when he entered my life and pointed out what was missing. He was able to crack the outer shell and in essence, introduce me to a side of myself I'd never met before. This allowed me to tap into a reserve of confidence I was previously unaware of. It was as close to feeling invincible as I'd ever come.

When his heart stopped beating, I was sent plummeting from the pedestal our bond had placed me on. I landed hard, surrounded by shattered pieces of my hopes and dreams. Broken and completely lost, I was a far cry from the lady his love had helped usher in.

Making my way along the twisted road of despair, I emerged from the darkness with a renewed commitment. I decided to rise in triumph, rather than be defined by tragedy. There is so much living to be done, one of many lessons learned in our time together. Tyger loved telling me we had to "get it all in" and now I am doing it for both of us.

Publishing my first book was a huge leap into the unknown. I trusted my instincts and the feeling that it was something I was meant to do. The Universe continues to confirm how right I was. From there, I began speaking in front of crowds, sharing intimate details of my personal life without fear of judgment. There couldn't be anything more out of character for me than this, yet here I am, standing up in front of the room like I was born to do it.

As I progress it's as though layers are being stripped away. Each one is a representation of different levels of fear: concern for what others might think or say, worries about looking foolish, being afraid of failing, and stubbornly holding onto old ideas that no longer serve my greatest good.

I fully embrace the concept that our souls entered these physical bodies in order to experience all the wonderful things life on earth has to offer. I'm sure we were aware of the contrast we'd face at times, but I believe we took on the challenge willingly, with the intent of conquering any obstacle. My acceptance of this allows me to see several areas of my life from a wider perspective. I've begun to reconsider what I once thought was set in stone.

During my first spiritual reading, the medium relayed Tyger's desire that I allow a new man into my life. Tyger said he wanted me to be with someone who would love me and be supportive. He added his hope that I allow this person to help ease my financial burden because he didn't want me to struggle. Tyger's sentiments were kind and noble, but fell on deaf ears.

My immediate reaction was, "no way." I wasn't prepared to hear anything close to that and I shook my head "no" even before the message was completely delivered. Later that evening, I had a long talk with Tyger and explained why this simply wasn't an option. Starting over with someone new was the furthest thing from my mind. My heart was consumed by our love and my desire to be with him. I dug my heels in and refused to budge. In fact, I said to him, "You'll have to accept this is how it is."

The case was closed, as far as I was concerned.

Now, I find myself considering what I'd previously thought impossible. Perhaps Tyger was right and there is room in my world for romance. Let me be clear... I am not actively searching for a relationship and I certainly don't spend my days longing to be with another. It isn't anything remotely close to that. What I am saying is, I'm at least open to the idea. I've gone from a fast no to a slow yes on the prospect of finding love again.

I'm not a stranger to male attention and a few have expressed interest in getting to know me. There have been offers of dinner or movie dates, but I've politely declined. I have no desire to join the dating scene and I'm not pining away in loneliness. I'm content with my own company. Writing is enjoyable and keeps me busy, as does promotional work for my book. There is so urgent need to embark on a search for "Mr. Right."

When and if we cross paths, it will happen naturally. It won't be forced or rushed at all. I believe whoever he is, we'll recognize one another by our energy. It will be a feeling beyond physical attraction that leaves us both incapable of resisting. My heart knows Tyger will have a hand in bringing him into my life, in some roundabout way. I'll be able to sense Tyger's involvement and know I have his blessing. There isn't any logical explanation for my awareness of any of this, but I'm absolutely sure.

Anyone who read my first book will remember how vehemently I stated, in no uncertain terms, there would never be another for me. When I spoke those words, I meant them. As I advance in the awakening process, understanding of my purpose has expanded. A major component is a willingness to embrace opportunities. After all, I signed up for this journey intending to absorb every facet of joy there is. Tyger and I share a bond that was formed long before we connected as sentient beings and will continue into eternity.

Feelings of jealousy, pride, and ego are left behind when we shed our physical bodies. Those emotions simply do not exist outside the human experience. Knowing this, there is no reason to feel as though I'm betraying Tyger by considering the possibility of connecting with another. I'm sure Tyger is extremely pleased with my new outlook. During his time here, my well-being was a top priority and his words from beyond the veil confirm that hasn't changed. Tyger always has my best interests at heart.

Our loved ones on the other side can see tomorrow much clearer than we can see today. I imagine Tyger looking out across the vast landscape and gently directing me toward sources of happiness. I have no doubt he is actively pulling strings, removing obstacles and opening doors for me. In this life, Tyger was a no-nonsense guy, who knew how to get things done. Once he figured out how things work in the afterlife, he resumed his role as the ultimate strategist. I've never met anyone who had a greater ability to get things done than Tyger. He will never miss an occasion to lift me higher or bring a smile to my face. I trust and welcome his guidance.

There is a whole planet to explore and so much I'd like to see and do. For the first time ever, I'm giving serious thought to moving away from my hometown. I've actually entertained the notion of relocating out of state. This is another one of those things I swore I'd never do. Finding my voice has led to a sense of freedom, a desire to see what's out there, beyond my limited scope. Obviously, this would require funding and I'm not quite in a position to pack up yet. The timeframe isn't as important as my openness to the idea.

Having spent my entire life in the town of my birth, I never saw a reason for leaving. This is where my family is and I'm comfortable here. Now, I find myself looking toward new horizons, curious as to what's around the next bend. With today's technology, it's easier than ever to remain connected across great distances. The old excuses for staying have lost their validity. I'm ready to follow the calling of my spirit and go where it leads.

Traveling has also piqued my interest. On my bucket list are several landmarks I plan to visit, across the United States. The Grand Canyon is at the top with Niagara Falls and Mount Rushmore close behind. I want to dip my toes in the Pacific Ocean one day, as well as spend time at Yellowstone National Park. Cruising the Caribbean is in my future as is a cruise of the Scandinavian countries. At least one stop on every continent would also be a dream come true.

These thoughts excite me as they enter my mind. The girl who once preferred to remain behind the scenes is now ready to take chances and step outside of her sheltered world. My time as a caterpillar has ended and the butterfly has emerged. I'm eager to dive into the fullness of life and climb far above my past inhibitions. The view from here is nothing short of spectacular.

As stated in this anonymous quote, "Life is not measured by the number of breaths we take but by the number of moments that take our breath away."

It's never too late to begin.

Chapter Sixteen
Visual Effects

I AM HIGHLY SENSUAL, always have been. My senses play a key role in my thoughts and every decision. Even more important than sight, smell, taste or sound is the way something makes me feel. It can be almost maddening sometimes but I'm unable to rest until whatever it is I'm working on falls into rhythm with my inner being.

This is why it takes me forever to put up the Christmas tree. The ornaments have to be placed in a harmonious way. My children learned at a young age, not to bother asking to help. Their mom turned trimming the tree into a serious project, so it was best to leave her alone. Yes, I realize this sounds terrible, but had I allowed them to assist. I would've moved everything anyway, as soon as they went to bed. May as well avoid wasting their time, is how I see it. Of the hours it takes me to complete this task, I'd estimate twenty percent is spent decorating and the other eighty involves me staring at each piece until my emotions signal their approval.

This carries over into other areas of my life, as well. Selecting which font to use when I'm writing usually takes far longer than it should. Why? Well, because it has to register someplace deep within that it fits. This is the case when creating covers for my books. It's as though I have an idea of exactly how I'd like the words to appear, except I can't provide a description. All I know for sure is I'll recognize it when I see it.

This becomes a painstaking, time consuming (and at times, frustrating) process as I scroll and click until the perfect lettering pops up. It may sound as though I'm describing some sort of obsessive/compulsive behavior but it isn't that. I am fully capable of making quick decisions in most areas of my life. I don't operate in a state of anxiety or fear in any form. There is no other way I can explain this trait, other than to say some things have to emit the right vibe and I won't be able to sign off until that happens.

I speak often about the manifestation process and our ability to attract into our lives what we wish for most. It certainly has worked for me on more than one occasion and I continue to apply the principles toward goals I have for the future. The Universe is aware of my aspirations because I've verbalized them. I believe wholeheartedly in my worthiness to receive what I've asked for and remain grateful for what I already have. Not so long ago I wanted to become an author who would inspire others and I continue to watch in amazement as it takes place before my eyes.

A major component involved in creating our own realities is the ability to see the object as belonging to us before it comes to fruition. This is the area I find somewhat troublesome. I have no problem forming a picture in my mind as having my desires; the issue lies in sustaining the thought. Since I struggle to keep the idea active, I find it difficult to arrive at a place of feeling as though it's already mine.

For a while, I'd been reading about the effectiveness of a posting your dreams on a vision board. If you've never heard of this, it's a collection of images and phrases which represent what you want most. As I do with most things, I dedicated a fair amount of time investigating how to best go about creating one.

Originally, I planned to cut pictures from magazines depicting what I'm striving to achieve. Since I don't receive subscriptions, this would mean purchasing various editions, hoping to find what was needed. The task seemed daunting which delayed my start. After a few weeks of going back and forth, I decided to make a digital version, using images from the Internet. It soon became clear, this was the right way to go.

The first step was figuring out exactly what I most wanted to envision. I narrowed it down to career, lifestyle, and travel. This gave me an outline to use in my search. I downloaded images relevant to being a successful author and speaker. Each one was chosen based on the level of inspiration invoked by seeing them. Next, I poured over thumbnails of houses, both interior and exterior, before locating those suited to my taste. The same methods were applied to choosing a vehicle. Finally, I obtained colorful graphics of places I would like to visit and that part of the project was complete.

Turning once again to GIMP, the image manipulation software used to create my book covers, I began assembling what I'd acquired. In addition to the photos, I added motivational phrases. This wasn't something to be rushed through, so I was particular right down to the last detail. Nothing was taken lightly, including the color schemes used to accentuate the words and their placement in key locations.

Studying my finished work, I felt the same elation that comes when the Christmas décor is to my liking. "This is it," I whispered to myself. "I can feel myself having this life."

Within seconds of viewing my creation, there is a rush of excitement as I pull into the driveway and remove the keys from the ignition of my dream car. Proceeding up the walkway and entering the front door of my contemporary-style bungalow, I am able to visualize making my way through the beautiful kitchen which flows into the huge living and dining area. Tossing my purse on the large, overstuffed chair in the corner, I begin prepping vegetables for the evening meal. Pausing briefly to click on the stereo, I'm off to the bedroom to change clothes. I can smell the fresh sheets on the king-sized bed in the master suite, as the warmth of the fireplace lets off a cozy glow. My home is comfortable and inviting.

Turning my attention to another area of the board, I am instantly transported to Barnes and Noble in Manhattan. There I am, ready to take my seat. The line is long, each person holding a copy of my latest book, patiently waiting to have it signed. I'm mindful of making eye contact and smiling at everyone, full of appreciation for their willingness to attend. The anticipation of hearing various accounts of contact they've had with loved ones from beyond the veil has my heart racing with excitement. I'm eager to engage with these strangers who speak the familiar language of similar experiences.

Setting my sights on the opposite corner of my compilation, I discover I'm not one bit nervous as the studio personnel fit me with a microphone in preparation for my interview with Oprah. It's hard to describe how ready I am for this, especially considering the majority of my existence has been plagued by shyness. None of that is present; I'm concentrating on telling my story and the many souls who need to know they're not alone in what they're going through. As I wait to begin, my only notion is, "I was built for this."

Glancing to the top right corner of the frame, I'm awestruck by the majesty and sheer power of nature on my visits to the Grand Canyon and Niagara Falls. The rush is almost indescribable as I take in the glory of these wonders. Thoughts flood my mind of the many times I'd seen them on TV and wished for a chance to be there in person. The reaction is identical as I board the ship for my cruise. I stand on the deck with the wind blowing through my hair, mesmerized by the view of nothing but ocean for as far as the eye can see. There is so much to do and I plan to get as much of it in as I possibly can. The trip is filled with nonstop fun from start to finish.

Every ounce of the jubilation I just shared was brought on by images laid out on an ordinary sheet of photo paper. After a few seconds of concentration, I was ready to kick myself for not having done this sooner. I'd been dragging my feet over sorting through magazines when everything I needed was right at my disposal, all along. I'm blown away by the intense emotional response to seeing my dreams laid out before me. I previously considered my energy level high but this incredible tool has launched it clear into the stratosphere. Each night when I lay my head on the pillow, several minutes are spent immersing myself in each section and acknowledging the reality of it all. This is my life I'm staring at and it already exists. The physical manifestation is on its way.

A fair amount of my amazement stems from recalling the person I became right after Tyger's death. Hopeless, downhearted, forlorn, dejected, mournful; any one of those words, or a combination of all, describes who I was. There was no planning for the future and the mere suggestion of making it to old age angered me. Every waking moment seemed pointless and without meaning.

Fast forward to the woman I am today, overloaded with ambition and confidence; approaching each new day with optimism. This boost is a result of seeing the wonderful possibilities life has to offer, colorfully displayed in clear view. I find myself feeling grateful not only for what I already have, but also for what's to come. It's a unique sensation when you can appreciate events that have yet to occur.

I'm sure there are some naysayers who'll claim a vision board is no more than child's play or fantasy. They'll declare it the equivalent of adults participating in a game of make-believe. I respectfully disagree with that opinion. The fact that I am now a published author, having had no knowledge of how to accomplish this, demonstrates the power of manifesting desires into reality. The process is valid and has been proven to me beyond the shadow of a doubt. How much faster will my goals materialize now that I can actually feel the effects of already reaching them? I'm convinced it will be sooner than I've yet dared to imagine.

I challenge you to give it a try. Find a quiet location where you can be alone with your thoughts. Ask yourself some serious questions. They'll vary depending on each situation but the basic ones should be, "What do I want to do with my life? What steps can I take right now, to get me closer? How much do I have to be grateful for in this exact moment? What obstacles (real or imagined) am I allowing to hold me back? What makes others more worthy of living their dreams than I am?"

Once you decide on real answers, gather whatever you can find to take you to a place of embracing this life as being yours. Visualization is an extraordinary thing. Remember what I shared earlier: the frontal lobe does not differentiate between the feeling of already having our desires and simply imagining we do. Let go of what society has repeatedly labeled as being "normal" and you'll open yourself up to the possibilities of the Universe, which science has conclusively proven to be infinite.

I literally feel as though the world is at my fingertips. There is no mountain too high or river too wide to keep me from succeeding in all I do. This absence of doubt infuses my spirit with courage and drives me far beyond what I once felt capable of. Reaching for the moon isn't nearly enough now that I know I have unlimited access to all there is. There is nothing to stop me except fear, and for me, it no longer exists.

Onward and upward it is.

Chapter Seventeen
Spreading the Wealth

AS MY STORY UNFOLDS, I continuously find myself in new territory. In my mind, I'm an apprentice, actively engaged in acquiring knowledge along an ever-widening path. Quite unexpectedly, I've also assumed the role of mentor. This isn't something I sought out, the opportunity presented itself and I am more than willing to oblige.

There is a quote, most often attributed to Pablo Picasso, which reads: "The meaning of life is to discover your gift and the purpose is to give it away." These words hold such truth. A close friend pointed out the diversity in my personal narrative and myriad of lessons I could potentially share with others. To quote what was said, "Diane, your story isn't only about overcoming grief. It includes accounts of your upbringing, the ambitious approach you took toward learning about writing and publishing, your ability to conquer the fear of public speaking, and so much more. A variety of audiences will be able to relate to you."

I had never considered any of that. My intent has always been helping the bereaved. It hadn't occurred to me these other aspects could be sources of inspiration as well. I'm an unassuming person; never considered myself as having been through more trials than anyone else. While that may be true, I've come to realize there is a benefit to gaining an understanding of how another has managed to overcome obstacles. I recognized early on, the healing effects of relatable experiences in regards to the loss of a loved one. For the first time, I was able to see the implications when applied to a broader spectrum.

I am honored every time someone reaches out with a question. Several have inquired as to what's involved in writing and publishing. Multiple acquaintances have shared their longtime interest in becoming authors and how they have incredible stories to tell. Prior to the release of my book, they hadn't been ready to take the next step. For the first time, they felt comfortable enough to advance. This came about as a result of my transformation. Motivation is being found by observing my emergence from the darkness with a renewed sense of purpose.

My reaction is the same each time I'm approached: overwhelming joy. There is no greater feeling than hearing someone describe their dreams and knowing your actions gave them the courage to get the ball rolling. This has nothing to do with pride or ego. It stems from a heartfelt desire to see another soul find their way and be successful in the process.

Others have told me of endeavors they thought about undertaking but were struggling to get off the ground. They wondered if I'd had any fears and what my mindset was, prior to putting pen to paper. Basically, these requests were for tips on how to get past this stumbling block. The value placed on my input is humbling, as it displays their confidence in my methods and achievements. I'm mindful of my responses, thinking long and hard before answering.

In one such case, I was aware of difficulties experienced by a particular person, and all they had overcome in the past. I offered the following advice, based on forward motion. *"I suggest you reflect on how far you've come from your darkest days and the fearless steps you've already taken toward improving your life. Keep that momentum going and take every step in faith. Even if things don't go exactly as you envision, you'll come away with valuable lessons learned, to apply on your next attempt or venture. You can accomplish anything your heart desires. Follow that inner voice and block out the external noise from others."*

I would provide the same counsel to anyone considering taking a risk. There is nothing to lose and everything to gain. No time like the present to begin when failure does not exist. Navigating a few potholes on the road to achievement is far better than a lifetime spent in the pit of regret. If getting to where you want to be means keeping your goals to yourself, then by all means, do so. Never let the doubts and fears of others douse the spark of your imagination. I applied this principle and had a published book in my hands before anyone had an opportunity to tell me why it wasn't possible. Fan your own flames by believing wholeheartedly in whatever you wish to accomplish.

I take pleasure in promoting the efforts of others. I happily share the work of authors, even those whose stories closely mirror my own. Anyone who perceives this as helping the competition may define this practice as self-destructive. There couldn't be anything further from the truth. We rise by lifting others, so each time I celebrate the victory of another it elevates me also. For far too long, man has operated under the assumption that there is a limit on abundance. A general consensus exists, which views successfulness as something to be hoarded, gathered up and stowed away. This logic is flawed on many levels.

The Universe has unlimited supplies of health, happiness, wealth, knowledge, and success. One person's ability to draw on this doesn't reduce the surplus for the rest of us. Applaud their achievements and you'll be tapped into the same flow. Similar to a bank account, you can't make constant withdrawals and expect the balance to replenish itself. A deposit is required. In Universal language, the "deposit" is made by offering encouragement and giving of ourselves. The light of one candle is not dimmed through the lighting of another. Instead, it is doubled in luminosity, brightening the way for the rest of us to follow.

It is my belief that we are all teachers and students. There is something to be learned from every encounter. Even interactions we find unpleasant come with a lesson. In the very least, what we attain from difficult people is how not to behave. Engaging with those who have completely different thought processes can be enlightening. It's amazing how looking at the same set of circumstances has the potential to result in views that are nothing alike. Hearing an alternate opinion often leads to healthy dialogue and expands our thinking. This is contingent, of course, upon both parties being open and willing to listen.

If there are skills I possess that can help educate another, I feel a responsibility to pass them along. Not with a boastful, "I know more than you do" attitude, but with a sincere willingness to aid in their advancement. A great deal of time went into researching every aspect of completing my book but input from others played a significant part as well. I received expert advice and answers from individuals who had no other motive except a desire to see me succeed. My determination to share what I've learned is not only a choice, but an obligation. The Universe is watching to see if I "pay it forward" and it's my privilege to do so.

Wouldn't it be wonderful if my words or actions became the catalyst to someone becoming a best-selling author, or world-famous clothing designer? The answer is an unequivocal, yes. In addition to my delight over their achievements, there is the added bonus of the blessings this attracts into my own life. Competing with others in some imagined contest for acquisitions or accolades is a pointless exercise. When love is the motivator and all-inclusive success is the goal, everybody wins.

I'm aware of the discouraging types who make it their mission to tear down rather than build up. This has little to do with the object of the attack. Its origin is actually rooted in recognition by the perpetrator of what they themselves lack. Most often displayed as jealous, envious behavior, it can escalate into a campaign to at most, destroy, or at least, tarnish, the reputation of another. I wish I could say I've never been subjected to this, but that isn't the case.

How does one react when their character is being called into question? For me, the initial response was shock. Shortly after releasing *Onward,* a Facebook friend left a confusing comment on one of my posts. Earlier in the day, my coworkers had presented me with a beautiful pen. It's pink (my favorite color) with my name and "Author" engraved in gold. This was a congratulatory gift to be used in future book signings. I was so appreciative and couldn't wait to get home and share a photo of it with my friends.

I was unprepared for one of the many replies which read, "Are the proceeds of the book going to charity?"

Wait a minute… was this person implying my intent in sharing my grief journey was an attempt to profit from Tyger's death?

No matter how much I tried to make sense of it, this appeared to be the only logical explanation for the question. Judging by the ensuing responses by those coming to my defense, I wasn't the only one who'd interpreted it this way.

Those words stung. It had never occurred to me that anyone could possibly be thinking this way. As I processed the situation, I soon realized how insignificant the opinion was. The most important reaction to the announcement of my book came from Tyger's relatives. Each of them expressed enthusiasm and gave their blessing, as did my own family. Therefore the implication behind this one statement could only affect me if I allowed it and I refused.

I've also heard rumors of negative remarks made by people around town. Whisperings to the effect of, "Who does she think she is, writing a book? Doesn't she know her man was this or that?" Again, I choose to not only ignore the gossip but also the person who felt the need to relay it. I chalk it up to a feeble attempt at distracting me from my purpose or to somehow diminish the positive impact being made on so many. It comes down to allowing myself to be pulled into a cesspool of negativity or remain in my peaceful state. The latter is the obvious choice.

In both cases, the human factor played a role in my initial reaction. I was hurt not only by what was said, but the intent behind it. The good news is the pain was short-lived. My energy was soon redirected toward the lives being touched and healing facilitated through the telling of the ordeal I'd managed to survive. The utterings of small minds pale in comparison to the hope being restored to many hearts. As I continue moving forward, there is the possibility of future occurrences such as these. That certainly doesn't deter me from my mission of helping others.

I've included these events to reiterate how possible it is to shield ourselves from the poisonous arrows of what many refer to as "haters." Tyger was grateful for them; he always gauged how well he was doing according to their level of interest. The more comments they made, the better things must've been going for him. If he were doing poorly, they'd have nothing to satisfy their need to see him fail. I now have an understanding of his philosophy and it bolsters my refusal to entertain drama of any sort.

Each time I'm approached by someone who is seeking information on how to proceed with an idea, it confirms I'm exactly where I belong. No one meets by accident. When paths cross, one is the student and the other the teacher. If these relationships continue, the roles become interchangeable and both parties grow. We have a duty to guide one another and offer direction when needed. This becomes increasingly evident, as I recall the advisements of my parents. I may not have always listened then, but much of what was spoken has had a lasting effect and a definite influence on who I am today.

The gifts we possess are meant to be shared. We each have something that could enhance someone else's life. You never know who could benefit from an ability that comes naturally to you and your success could inspire countless others. I can say with absolute certainty, there are witnesses to my evolution who are finding the courage to take chances on reaching goals they previously felt were out of reach.

As I come into my own with my natural talent, it's important to help others develop theirs as well. This is done by answering questions, giving suggestions, and offering tips and insights. I accept that none of us has all the answers and there is always more to be learned. It's through this exchange of information that we reach our full potential.

This generosity of spirit and a willingness to pool individual strengths is beneficial to us all. The easiest way to access abundance is by relinquishing the need to conceal our inner greatness. In the words of Buddha, "You only lose what you cling to."

The power lies in letting go.

Chapter Eighteen
The Human Factor

I CONSIDER MYSELF TO BE FULLY ENGAGED in my spiritual awakening. I've acquired a multitude of methods for staying focused and tools to aid in accomplishing goals. My knowledge of Universal law is applied on a consistent basis. I can say with confidence, I have a firm grasp on what it takes to manifest my heart's desires from concepts to reality.

With such a well-stocked arsenal of information, you'd think my days were spent chasing butterflies in a meadow of rainbows. Perhaps you've conjured up images in your mind of me living as free as the wind, without a care in the world. That all sounds lovely, but it's definitely not the case. While I feel grateful and do my best to accentuate the positives, the fact remains I am limited in this physical form, as we all are. Ego and pride still rear their bothersome heads from time to time and I am in no way immune to their effects.

What has changed is how long I allow myself to remain in that space. Thanks to all I've learned, I'm acutely aware of the damaging effects of any form of insecurity. Negative feelings are acknowledged and processed but I don't pitch a tent and live there. The key is to move through it as swiftly as possible, then redirect the energetic flow to a spirit of well-being.

Because expressing appreciation is such a high priority for me, attention is seldom given to lack. Financially I'd describe myself as stable. My income covers the bills, although some months this involves a fair amount of juggling. Extravagant meals aren't currently in the budget, but we're far from the point starvation. I don't entertain stress, but on the rare occasion when it makes its presence known, money is usually involved in some way.

The winter months can be particularly challenging with the added expense of heating the apartment. This isn't included in the rent so I'm responsible for purchasing oil to keep us warm and supplied with hot water. Even with the board collected from my sons and their help, difficulties arise. After running out of fuel a few times over the years, I grew tired of paying the delivery person extra money to bleed the line in order to start the furnace. The final straw was the day a woman driver showed up and I let her into the basement to get the boiler going. My take on that was if she could do it, so could I.

Searching YouTube, I watched tutorials and discovered it was actually quite simple. Following the steps, I held my breath as I hit the red reset button. The excitement that followed when I heard the "whoosh" and saw the orange flame ignite was off the charts. Let's just say it involved some jumping up and down and a huge sense of accomplishment.

I've become adept at stretching my dollars well beyond what seems possible. This often means prioritizing the bills and spending. If purchasing a bulk amount of oil isn't an option on a particular week, then it's off to the gas station for diesel every few days. For anyone who isn't aware, this is a viable alternative. The product used for home heating is exactly the same except a reddish dye is added to it. It's a matter of filling my five-gallon can at the pump, then pouring it into the fill pipe on the side of the house.

To some, this may sound like a burden or terrible struggle. From my perspective, the minor inconvenience of transporting fuel to limp us along is outweighed by the prospect of a nice, hot shower. In other words, I'm grateful. Circumstances aren't ideal when this occurs, but could be far worse. Through it all, I maintain an unwavering faith of arriving at a place in life where all of this is no more than a distant memory. Until then, I will continue to do what's necessary.

In situations pertaining to me or the household bills, there is little, if any, anxiety. The issues arise when I'm unable to offer assistance to my sons. They are hardworking and neither one expects a handout. Both are humble, unassuming and understand the need to earn a living. I look on in amazement at their "above and beyond" approach. When adversity strikes they meet it head-on; an admirable quality they each possess. Their personalities are quite different but this is one trait they have in common.

Aaron, my oldest, walked a considerable distance to and from work for several weeks while he was without a vehicle. He declined my offers of a ride, stating it was his responsibility and he was too old to expect his mom to drive him around. Despite my best efforts to assure him I didn't mind, he refused to accept.

As a mother, this was difficult to watch. On one hand, I was proud of his conviction and work ethic. On the other, it pained me to think of him going such a great distance on foot, in every type of weather imaginable. I respected his decision and it paid off when he was able to purchase a reliable car. Through it all, I admired his independence and determination to make his own way.

My second born was operating under similar circumstances. In addition to attending community college, Mark was working two part-time jobs. His goal was to save up for a vehicle and was undeterred even after failing his first attempt at getting his driver's license. He passed the second time but his funds weren't yet sufficient. This meant he was still forced to ride public transportation frequently. When my work schedule permitted, I would either let him use my car or pick him up after his shifts.

His father, my ex-husband, has always been a wonderful provider for our son. I communicated to him how hard Mark was working and he decided to send the money for a used car. Mark and I located something affordable and his dad initiated a wire transfer to cover the full purchase price. Mark paid for his own insurance and we obtained his ID card as proof of coverage, the night before the car was to be registered. I was so happy for my son; finally, he would have the freedom of being able to get around on his own.

My joy soon turned to nervous apprehension when I realized we had miscalculated the total cost of registration and sales tax. Mark had put most of what he had toward the down-payment for insurance and wasn't able to afford the added expense. His father had sent this lump sum only days before and I had no resources to pull from.

I began feeling physically ill at the idea of having to tell my son we wouldn't be able to proceed right away. He was at work, anticipating being handed his keys the following day. I had sent him a text after printing his ID cards, letting him know the vehicle was officially covered. The thought of disappointing him was almost too much to bear. I sat in silence, nursing a massive headache and upset stomach. Finally, I decided to do the only thing I could think of, place a call to his dad and see if he could help.

When he answered the phone, I began pouring out my despair. He listened quietly and when I allowed him to speak, his response was simple. "Give me an exact amount and I'll send it." I thanked him profusely and we ironed out the particulars before ending the call. The crisis had been averted.

This should've filled me with relief, yet it did little to alleviate my anxiety. What I was experiencing following the call was more in line with guilt and failure. Rather than direct my attention toward his father providing for Mark, I sat immersed in my own inadequacy. After all, he has two parents. Why wasn't I able to help out? When would I ever be in a position to give my sons a little boost in life? My parents had helped me get on my feet in my younger years. Why did everything fall on his father's shoulders? Questions were swirling in my head, adding to the throbbing pain being caused by tension.

This entire scenario was my doing. His dad hadn't uttered one word that would indicate he was concerned about being taken advantage of. Yet this is how I was feeling. Father or not, he has bills and responsibilities like everyone else. As a mother, I should've been able to contribute. There was no shaking it and I was becoming consumed by a self-inflicted sense of lack. The dominant thought in my mind? Diane, you suck as a parent.

The only remedy I could come up with was to shut things down for the night and go to bed. I was caught up in this gloominess so in order to escape it I decided to sleep and have faith in a better tomorrow. Before sliding under the covers, I positioned my vision board in the usual spot on the nightstand. Rather than scroll through Facebook, which was the normal routine before closing my eyes, I studied the images. My dreams, aspirations, and goals were depicted in living color; representations of abundance. Completely engrossed in the beauty of this reality, I repeated, "This is my life" before turning off the lamp and quietly drifting off.

When I awakened the following morning, I was back to my optimistic self. My spirit was recharged and fully equipped to handle any challenges the new day would bring. I turned my attention away from what I hadn't been able to do and toward my ex-husband's willingness to help our son. I thought about Mark's excitement and the independence of having his own transportation. Gratitude flowed from my heart for the ability of his dad and me to communicate and co-parent our son with no residual discontent from the past. I recalled the searches I'd done for insurance quotes and the time spent locating a reliable vehicle in an affordable price range. The responsibility fell to me since his dad lives in another part of the country. Financially, I hadn't been able to contribute, but I assisted in other important areas. This had been a joint effort after all.

We received the additional funds and Mark was soon driving himself wherever he needed to go. The smile on his face was more than enough to let me know I hadn't failed him. He was thankful to have had the help of both parents and expressed that to each of us. Wishing I'd been able to do more hadn't hindered the outcome.

As my dreams continue to manifest and finances improve, my sons will reap the benefits along with me. Over the years we've had good periods and bad. We rejoice in prosperity and rally together during lean times. Up or down, we support one another. Their willingness to make a way for themselves gives me all the more reason to share my successes with them. Our day is coming and I tell them this often.

My inability to help Mark with his car invoked a melancholy reaction. I've included this to show how my enlightened state doesn't serve as an impenetrable shield for every hardship that comes along. I'm subject to blue moods, like anyone else. What it does do is keep me from becoming stuck in one gear. The promise of better circumstances is strong enough to prevent me from falling into a pattern of "woe is me." Demonstrating my vulnerability as a human being is just as important as sharing positive achievements. This serves as an example that even the occasional lapse into old thought patterns doesn't derail the manifestation process.

There is a line from the movie "Pirates of the Caribbean" where Johnny Depp's character, Captain Jack Sparrow says, "The problem is not the problem. The problem is your attitude about the problem." Someone made this into a meme which resurfaces every so often on social media. It resonates with me each time it graces my newsfeed because of the truth it contains.

I consider this quote to be a perfect summation of what we inflict upon ourselves by overthinking. I've come quite far in getting to know my authentic self, yet I still succumb to it occasionally. While navigating the path to enlightenment we all encounter the occasional pothole or bump in the road. Periodic sadness or disappointment are part of the human experience and shouldn't be suppressed. Instead of beating yourself up over a bad day, do your best to get through it, let it go, and continue on. We can use those experiences to grow and emerge stronger, better equipped to handle future storms. There is no perfect awakening, it's about being open, receptive and keeping the faith.

The fact that I take a positive approach to life doesn't mean I pretend things are good every second of the day. Seeing the bright side doesn't involve burying my head in the sand and refusing to acknowledge the shady areas. There are times my ability to handle hardships is put to the test. I find the quickest way to get past it is by listening to the voice of reason from within, assuring me "this too shall pass." We have a tendency to drown out this advice by attempting to justify our right to feel bad. This is soon followed by the pity party and before we know it we're cascading down the slippery slope of self-doubt, headed straight for misery.

I've trained myself to pump the brakes before reaching the point of no return. Those gentle words of wisdom are signals from the soul; reminders that we are bigger than any problem, regardless of how insurmountable it may seem. As with all things in life, it comes down to a choice.

When Tyger died, my first inclination was to give up. Consumed by grief, I was nearly defeated. The promise of hope found its way in and I nurtured it. Instead of shouting over the inner whisperings, telling me to push on, I bought into the message. From there it was a matter of entertaining the prospect of overcoming my sorrow and making it a reality.

This approach is taken in the face of every obstacle. Some are harder to conquer than others but surrender is not an option I choose to consider. The other side of happiness is a location we've all had the misfortune of visiting but is by no means, a place to live.

Chapter Nineteen
Kindred Spirits

THERE IS STRENGTH IN NUMBERS. I'll take that truth even further by saying there is immeasurable power in the collaboration of like-minds. As I continue moving forward, my circle is adjusted to include those whose energy either matches or intensifies my own. I am drawn to souls who are actively involved in becoming the best they've ever been, then continuing to reach for the next level.

Due to my trusting nature, I've been fooled a time or two by individuals who, on the surface, appear to be living with a positive mindset. Unfortunately, there are some who pretend well and over time their lower vibrations reveal themselves. My initial reaction is one of love and understanding. Every effort is made to improve their outlook by pointing out the bright side of any situation. There are some who are either unable or unwilling to move from this negative space.

My power of discernment continues to improve, allowing me to recognize those who fall into this category. When positive responses seem to be getting me nowhere, I wish them well and walk away. Prolonged interactions with these types are draining so it becomes necessary to cancel my subscription to their issues. This isn't done out of anger or from a retaliatory aspect. I simply recognize the value of protecting my peaceful state and making it a number one priority. The quality of my life experience takes precedence over the quantity of associates surrounding me.

In no way do I mean to imply this makes me somehow superior to anyone else. The only person I'm striving to be better than is the one I was yesterday. I am more than willing to share the lessons I've learned with anyone who is interested. There are some who aren't ready to receive the message. Since we are at differing stages of our journeys, I accept that and continue on my path.

There is an undeniable spark when we connect with others who mirror our vibration. Before long we begin to feed off of one another. The exchange of ideas is seamless and there is no resistance to receiving their message. Positivity builds up and is exchanged equally between parties, without any sense of disapproval.

I'm speaking of individuals who are genuinely pleased to witness the success of others. Their encouragement and willingness to share information is meant to elevate, rather than deflate, dreams and aspirations. Even when relaying an alternative view, their words are soothing. Support is given and direction is offered from a place of caring, without judgment. Should you choose not to accept their advice, they understand your right to do so.

This enlightened way of thinking is welcome in my world. The Universe continually places people in strategic places to help me advance or in some cases, shed a light on what's missing. The key to making this work is a willingness to listen. I feel blessed each time I come across a person like this.

Tyger was one of the greatest teachers I've ever had. He spoke the language of experience sprinkled with a heavy dose of common sense. Had it not been for him, I have no idea where I'd be. More than likely, it would involve contentment with the status quo and quietly going through the motions. Each day would consist of existing and calling it living.

In our time together, I felt alive and so did he. We could be engaged in the most routine, mundane task, yet it felt extraordinary because we were together. Every positive trait and attribute was amplified by the love we shared. This is the glow recognized by so many who knew us. They couldn't quite put their finger on it, but something was different about Tyger and Diane. An activity as simple as a long ride along a country road became an adventure because we were completely involved in the moment.

Neither of us sought to change anything about the other. We celebrated our individuality and independent natures. Between the two of us, we were introduced to a variety of experiences and perspectives. There was nothing condescending in our reactions to anything from the past. Tyger's zodiac sign was Leo, and he could roar like the king of the jungle, if provoked. One might expect this to be a recipe for disaster with a lady bull, such as myself but we shared a level of understanding that went deeper than any disagreement.

If asked to describe the strongest attribute of our relationship in one word, it would be respect. We shared a mutual admiration for what each of us brought to the table. Our focus was on accentuating the positives rather than dwelling on slight differences of opinion. We shared a common desire to see the other shine, to succeed in each new venture and excel in every achievement. This continues to occur as he watches me grow and expand my reach into new areas. Tyger is my greatest cheerleader, of this I have no doubt.

While revisiting our many discussions, I often come back to one of the most important questions he ever asked, "What is it that really makes Diane happy?" He stopped me in my tracks with that one. It required some thought as I realized it was the first time anyone had ever inquired. Tyger called attention to the fact that up until that point, I'd been going through the motions of surviving each day. There were moments of laughter and joy but I couldn't name one thing I did, solely for my own enjoyment. Everything was attached to the household, my children, or a significant other.

This was not a question I ever posed to him, yet our union also called attention to what he'd been missing. He began allowing me access to parts of him that had been off limits in previous relationships. Tyger gave me the best of himself and in our time together, we became better versions of ourselves than either of us had ever been.

Tyger's physical journey has ended, yet my respect and admiration for him continue on. One of many ways I honor his legacy is by refusing to remain frozen in time. There is a season for everything and I am no longer hindered by the crippling effects of grief. My wish to experience the fullness of life was originally driven by my commitment to him. It is now fueled by my acceptance that it's the only way to live and I'd be shortchanging myself by doing anything less.

Along with being receptive to guidance, I'm committed to sending positive energy to anyone in need of a boost. Even the most enlightened among us can be temporarily thrown off course by an unexpected storm. An encouraging attitude is sometimes all we need in order to press on. This is one of the main reasons I share my successes on social media. There may be someone on the verge of giving up who finds inspiration in an accomplishment of mine. Especially those who know the story of all I've been through prior to reaching this point.

I'm not what you'd consider a "fly by the seat of my pants" type of girl. I listen, observe, and do my homework. I respond to the callings of my soul and remain open to suggestions that resonate with my purpose. I avoid the dream killers and gravitate toward those motivated by self-improvement and actively engaged in expanding their personal awareness.

Scientists have studied the chemistry behind attraction and repulsion. There is evidence to support the irresistible effects of pheromones, or scent, unique to each individual. While I don't doubt the validity of their findings, speaking as a sensual person,

I prefer to follow my inner guidance system. To put it plainly, I trust my gut.

We've all had occasions of being in someone's presence and something felt "off." There is no logical explanation for it, but the atmosphere around them seems unsettled somehow. Then there are others who draw us in like magnets. For whatever reason, we feel a sense of peace while in their immediate vicinity. In both cases, we're tuned into the frequency being emitted and reacting accordingly.

With those we're drawn to, the blending of energies is something to behold. We feel "at home" in their presence and communicate easily. The familiarity seems to indicate we're acquainted on some deeper level. Often, when we encounter these individuals, the intensity is so great that others are pulled in as well. Suddenly people start smiling in our direction or joining in the conversation. The connection is extremely powerful and impossible to ignore.

While this can be the perfect recipe for romance (as with Tyger and me) it isn't always. This can occur between relatives, friends, coworkers, mentors, students, teachers or even a brief association. Regardless of the relationship, the arrangement is mutually beneficial.

I stumbled across the concept of "Soul Groups" in a book titled, Testimony of Light, by Helen Greaves. This story is an account of ADCs or "After Death Communications" Helen received from her close friend, Frances Banks. Prior to Frances' passing, she lived as an Anglican nun, who'd spent many years doing missionary work in South Africa. Helen began receiving messages after Frances died, and the book is a description of life beyond the veil.

This is one of the most detailed accounts I've ever read of what awaits us on the other side. Written as though Frances is speaking, the reader gets the sense of receiving first-hand knowledge. As profound as the message is, the method of delivery makes it even more believable. I place this at the top of my list of most impactful stories on the subject of the afterlife.

There is significant discussion of the various levels of existence souls encounter after shedding this physical form. The most enlightened inhabit the higher realms and become mentors to those who have yet to evolve to this point. As I read about this, it made far more sense than what I'd been taught by religion. The two choices of heaven or hell had always seemed so extreme. The concept of having an opportunity to improve through the counsel of an experienced soul appears more in line with a spirit of love than eternal damnation; at least, in my opinion.

"Soul Groups" are explained as being a collective who come into the earthly plane with a unified purpose. Some choose to incarnate as part of the same family, in order to develop a bond as relatives. Others enter into contracts where they agree to meet up at some point in order to accomplish a goal for the betterment of all. As our physical journeys advance, we have no memory of the agreement yet we are able to recognize one another, even if it's on a subconscious level. I find this intriguing because it offers an explanation for the familiarity felt between myself and others, sometimes complete strangers, when there is no apparent reason for it.

I firmly believe Tyger and I are part of the same soul group. In one of his many messages since his transition, he said we agreed long ago to do something important together. This is in line with what I've read. There are several people I've identified as fellow group members, my goddaughter, Crystal, being one. The ease of communication between us and level of understanding we share has me convinced.

My trust is in the vibes I pick up from others. I rely on this far more than ever before. Words can be tailored to fit and actions modified, but energy doesn't lie. Kindred spirits bring warmth and helpful intentions. They are sources of inspiration who leave us feeling better about ourselves. I choose to surround myself with people of similar ideals and purpose.

Tyger taught me to make happiness a priority. He was an excellent teacher and remember, I'm a straight "A" student.

I am actively applying the lesson.

Chapter Twenty
All in the Approach

I DO MY BEST to stay in a receptive mode. Positive words, thoughts, and feelings are sown, with an expectation of reaping marvelous fruit. Generous amounts of faith and patience nourish the soil, allowing the seeds to take root. The crop is watered with gratitude; expressions of appreciation for all I have. From there I go about the business of living. Keeping constant watch is unnecessary and actually has a negative impact on growth.

Think of it this way. When a farmer plants corn, does he stand guard twenty-four hours a day waiting for the first sprout to emerge? Of course not. He does his part, then allows nature to take its course. This analogy is a representation of our behavior when something we're hoping for doesn't show up right away. Agonizing over the process directs energy toward the lack of obtaining what's desired and away from anticipation. It's best to leave things be and allow the Universe to handle the particulars.

This logic is tried and true. It's the method I used in order to get my first book published. The "how" wasn't my concern. I knew it had to be done and refused to be swayed by appearances. This is not an isolated incident or a random stroke of luck. It continues to occur and strengthens my belief each time.

Once a year, a group of my female cousins and I go away for what we call, "Sistas Weekend." It consists of a couple of nights spent together at a hotel. We stay fairly close to home but enjoy a well-deserved break from daily routines. No husbands, significant others or kids are allowed, and we have a blast.

We decided to do something different and plan a weeklong getaway in a city of our choosing. One of the girls owns a timeshare so that was her gift to us. We were each responsible for airfare and our own spending money but there would be no hotel costs. It didn't take long to select our destination; someone suggested Las Vegas and we unanimously agreed. The sistas were planning to take Sin City by storm.

The trip was scheduled for the following year, giving us time to save and locate decent flights that wouldn't break the bank. This was sure to be a great vacation and I was caught up in the excitement of the idea. It was several weeks before we needed to give our final answers on whether or not we'd be attending. The timeshare would have to be booked so we were required to give a definite yes or no.

The time that passed between discussing our plans, and actually having to commit, was long enough for me to drift back down to reality. I was still new to my job and adjusting to a reduced income. There was no surplus of funds or savings to tap into. I began to wonder why I ever thought going on this trip was a possibility. My brain stated in no uncertain terms, "You can't afford to go."

The following day, I received a group text. The accommodations were being finalized so a total headcount was needed. I was on my afternoon break at work, sitting outside at the wooden picnic table behind the building. Looking down at the phone in my hand, I knew what my answer had to be. I turned the device horizontally, to access the larger keyboard and began typing. My reply consisted of two words, "I'm in" before immediately hitting the send button.

"Wait," I said to myself. "What did I just do?"

The response to this question washed over me as an overwhelming sense of calm. My thoughts turned to Tyger and how he would've moved mountains to enable me to go. I imagined his joy at me doing something so spontaneous, so completely out of character. I was taking a chance and he was loving it. In that moment I knew there was no need to worry. By any means necessary, I would be on a flight with my cousins the following spring. The discussion was over and that was it.

As time progressed, I maintained my stance and firm belief of it being none of my business how this would happen. Life went on as usual and my outlook remained optimistic. A few months before the trip, a cousin had a lucrative night at a local casino. She generously offered to purchase one-way tickets for our flight to Vegas. This was her gift to us since the money had come unexpectedly. The rest of what I needed showed up in the form of an income tax refund that I hadn't anticipated receiving.

The message here? I had been concerned about covering the cost by drawing from my earnings and in the end, it had nothing to do with weekly wages. It flowed in effortlessly from unusual places and I couldn't have predicted it would unfold as it did. I followed my gut by confirming my attendance, then trusted the pieces to come together. I continued paying the household bills and took care of expenses without worrying about where the extra would come from. It showed up because I upheld my end of the bargain, and the Universe is always faithful.

We had a wonderful week of shopping, sightseeing and soaking up the ambiance. The gamblers among us went off to try their luck and the rest took part in our individual interests. My top priority was to lie by the pool with a refreshing cocktail; a feat I accomplished more than once. As a group, we took in a show, ate some great food, visited Madame Tussaud's Wax Museum and explored the strip. The highlight was our night in old Vegas for the Fremont Street Experience. This area is home to the original casinos from the early days and the streets are filled with vendors, performers, music, and some unexpected sights. Definitely not a place I'd bring children, but lots of fun for adults.

My gratitude for this amazing vacation continued after returning home. Witnessing the manifestation process first-hand is something to behold. I committed my mind to going with complete disregard for the means of it becoming a reality. This manifestation in itself was enough to solidify my commitment to living in gratitude, but there would be more to come.

Summer was approaching and I had requested a few days off in June, July, and August. Rather than take a full week all at once, I chose to extend my weekends during the warmer months. This would give me some much-needed beach time and I'd be able to go on weekdays when it wasn't as crowded.

In early June, Angy found herself in a predicament. My goddaughter, Crystal, who I spoke of earlier, is Angy's oldest daughter. Crystal's son, Andrew, had been here in Connecticut visiting his grandparents and would be returning to Florida soon. Angy's twins, Tiani and Terrell, were flying back with him to stay with their big sister for summer break. The twins were thirteen and Andrew a few years younger. Angy didn't feel comfortable having them travel without an adult, especially since she was struggling to find direct flights.

This was causing a dilemma since the restaurant had recently opened and neither Angy nor Dewayne could get away. Their resolution was to buy me a round trip ticket in order to fly down with the kids. I hesitated at the thought of them paying my way until Angy explained the expense would be the same, even if I chose not to go. The timing was such that she and Dewayne had to oversee the business, but should I decline, one of them would be forced to go. Regardless of my answer, a ticket needed to be purchased. By agreeing, I'd be doing them a favor.

An unexpected twist came when she told me the dates of the trip. I was shocked to hear the exact days I'd been approved for in July. I could hardly believe my ears. My selections had been made randomly since I had no plans. How in the world had this happened? Not only was I going on a free trip to Florida, I already had the time off from work. The Universe was screaming to me, so there was no choice but to say yes. I jokingly began referring to

Dewayne as the "Godfather of Barbecue" since they'd made me an offer I couldn't refuse.

I spent three days and two nights in the Sunshine state, relaxing amongst the palm trees and catching up with family. In the several years Crystal lived in Florida, this was my first time visiting. It seemed as though I was there much longer because we managed to do so much. Not one second felt rushed. We lounged by the pool, spent a day at the beach, and ate some delicious food at a neighborhood Mexican restaurant. A highlight for me was standing on the shore both nights, watching the breathtaking sunset.

There was the added bonus of seeing my cousin Lisa, as well as her children and grandchildren. Lisa and I had been extremely close growing up but since her relocation to Florida, we'd lost touch. Imagine my excitement at learning she lived less than thirty minutes from where I was staying. Lisa's oldest, Lakiesha, is also my goddaughter, along with Crystal and Angy's youngest girl, Tiani. Having all three of them together was unprecedented. We took some great photos and enjoyed one another. Gratitude filled my heart.

As 2016 drew to a close, I assessed my accomplishments for the year. A hard-working woman with limited resources had managed to become a published author, spend seven fabulous days in Las Vegas, and a summer holiday in Florida. The rent continued to be paid each month, utilities were on, the vehicle was maintained, and the cabinets never emptied. Don't get me wrong, there were weeks when the grocery budget delved into ramen noodle status but I ate every bite with the knowledge of my present situation not being my final destination. My attitude remained "better to have noodles than nothing at all" and I meant it.

This is my view on everything. There is always a bright side. It comes down to what we choose to focus on. The old adage applies, "Is the glass half empty or half full?" From my perspective, it is always half full. In either case, it's certainly refillable so it's never too late to embrace a new perception.

On a sunny Saturday afternoon in early fall, I drove my granddaughter to the football field. Sophia is a cheerleader and her mom wasn't able to get the day off, so she asked if I'd mind bringing her to the game. The girls needed to arrive early, so I explained to the coach I had to leave but would be back soon. Markie was in need of a ride to work, then I'd return.

Approaching my car, I noticed the rear driver's side tire appeared to be low on air. It was strange since it hadn't been driving differently. "Oh well," I thought. "I'll grab Markie then get air on the way to his job." By the time I got back to the house, it was nearly flat. I do have a spare but since neither of us had ever changed a tire, I hoped to make it to the closest gas station and attempt to inflate it.

It was a rough ride, but we made it. I could hear a hissing sound, as though the air was escaping, but it filled and seemed to be holding. Immediately after getting Mark to work, I went directly to the Tire and Lube center at Walmart. I explained the problem and the technician said depending on the condition, there was a possibility of plugging the hole. They took my vehicle right in and he assured me he'd be back in a few minutes to tell me how things looked.

After a short while, the polite young man requested I come out to see what had caused the issue. In his hand was a broken off drill bit, still attached to the shank—a piece of metal approximately two inches long and a quarter of an inch in diameter. This was what punctured my tire. His state of disbelief was nearly as great as mine. I expected him to find a nail or perhaps a screw, but how had something of this size become lodged in the tread? He also pointed out significant damage; a result of having driven with it practically flat. Contact with the rim had ground off a handful of rubber particles and caused wear on the outer wall. His next comment grabbed my attention. "Good thing you didn't drive on the highway. At those speeds, this tire would have blown."

What he didn't know was, that's exactly what I'd done. The quickest route to Walmart from where I'd been was the interstate, so I'd opted to go that way. My thoughts shifted to Tyger and I uttered a silent, "Thank you," for getting me safely to the repair shop.

It was obvious the tire was beyond help so I purchased a new one. The money had been earmarked for the cable bill which would now have to wait. The car had to come first since without it there would be no getting to work. After thirty minutes I was back on the road but not before asking to keep the object that caused the problem. It certainly wasn't something you'd typically find and I needed a visual reminder of this brush with danger.

It took a little while to fully digest what happened. My final assessment can be summed up in one word: Gratitude. There were so many opportunities for this scenario to have ended tragically. After all was said and done, it cost me the price of a new tire, which was needed anyway. Of the three people who'd ridden in the car, not one had been hurt. This incident could have easily occurred after I'd already paid the bills or an off week since my salary is deposited bi-weekly. The inconvenience was minimal and not even remotely worth dwelling on.

There is power in expectation. I remember a period in my life when my thinking was backward. If some major event was on the horizon which involved any uncertainty, my approach was to refrain from getting my hopes up. I'd even go as far as to expect it not to happen, in order to minimize the level of disappointment if it failed. I now realize how detrimental this outlook can be. Excited anticipation energizes the strength of attraction. There are no failures. The victory sometimes comes in unexpected forms and the lesson is often the most valuable component.

I arrive for every doctor's appointment fully expecting a good report. My employer provides medical insurance, so I keep up with wellness visits. This isn't done out of fear something may be wrong. The opposite is true. I live in a constant state of knowing all is well, so I enjoy the inner "I knew that already" of hearing good reports. There might be a slight touch of ego involved but it's more about confirmation than anything else.

During a physical with my primary physician, I quietly listened as she relayed the results of my recent blood work. In every category, the numbers were "better than good" (her choice of words.) She told me I should thank my great genetics. I'm sure that's part of it, but the most significant contributing factor is I do not entertain the thought of bad news. There is a chance of being told something other than I initially expected but how I receive it is what matters. There is a huge difference between assigning yourself a death sentence and being engaged in the lesson as you face a challenge head-on.

This has been the biggest area of growth on my relatively new journey of getting to know my true self. I have an insatiable hunger for life. I want to see farther, climb higher, hear clearer, feel deeper, and acquire as much knowledge as my brain can hold. I was broken when Tyger crossed over, devastated beyond belief. As the fractures heal, they become stronger than before. Each break is infused with the indelible qualities of hope and perseverance. The "why me" of self-pity has become the "why not me" of infinite possibilities.

While surfing the Internet, I came across a website featuring Connecticut authors. Right away I clicked on the link to join but found it had been disabled. As I searched for a number to call, I was redirected to a page announcing the reinstatement of the Connecticut Book Awards. That was an attention grabber, so I scanned the page to find out the requirements.

In order to qualify, the title had to have been published between January and December of 2016. The author was required to have resided in Connecticut for three successive years, been born there, or the story had to be set in the state.

"Oh, my goodness. My book meets the criteria." This realization caused an instant spike in my heart rate.

As I write these words, I have no idea of how *Onward into The Light* will fare. The one thing I'm absolutely certain of is the chances of winning are reduced to zero if I fail to enter. There is no downside to entering. I have no idea of the prize because to me any reward would pale in comparison to the honor of being recognized for my work. Of course, I would graciously accept any recognition that would come with having my book voted as the favorite in the category of non-fiction. All I'm saying is I am overjoyed by the opportunity to participate. Anything beyond that is icing on the cake.

In addition to creating our own realities, we also determine the atmosphere of our surroundings. Some will read this chapter and find inspiration in my outlook and accomplishments. Others won't be able to get past the idea of me occasionally eating ramen noodles for dinner. This is where choice comes into play. It's all in how we choose to see circumstances.

I am one who smiles and have been the majority of my adult life. I specify "adult life" because as a child, smiling was a rarity. My mother told a funny story of us walking downtown, to have professional photos taken at Sears. I was probably two, at the time. She was aware of my habit of non-compliance when a camera was involved. All the way there, she did her best to convince me how pretty my pictures would look if I did as the photographer asked. Apparently, I assured her there was nothing to worry about. "Yes, Mommy. I'll smile." This was my answer as we crossed the threshold and entered the store.

We arrived in the studio and that poor man did everything short of standing on his head to get me to curl my lips in an upward motion, but this stubborn Taurus child would not budge. No matter how many funny faces he made, silly sounds uttered, or toys offered, I sat unimpressed and stone-faced. Sensing his growing frustration and getting low on patience herself, my mother finally exclaimed, "Just go ahead and take the picture before she cries."

He did as he was asked and the finished product is a lovely portrait of a toddler, hair neatly styled in the cutest little pigtails, wearing a pink flowered dress and a Cinderella wristwatch, looking as sober as a judge. Every word of this is true but as the years passed, I developed a fondness for beaming happily.

If I had a dollar for every time I've been asked, "why are you always smiling?" I would be a wealthy woman. The question is usually posed as though there's something wrong with a happy expression. In most cases, I'm not even consciously aware of the smile on my face. It appears on its own; the effect of positive emotions coming to the surface. I'm taken aback by the tone which sometimes accompanies the inquiry. I sense the person is somehow annoyed by my joy.

From my perspective, I wonder why these individuals aren't smiling themselves. They can't find one reason to be jovial? In my opinion, the lack of happiness is an unnatural state. A genuine smile from a stranger can be the key to improving someone's entire day. We have no way of knowing what anyone is going through.

This is why I choose to be kind. It could literally make the difference between life and death. The cashier with the sad eyes may be contemplating suicide when she leaves work that evening. Suppose the reassurance of your smile is exactly what she needs to feel like someone cares. Whether or not she ever sees you again, is irrelevant. The fact that for one millisecond, another soul acknowledged her existence could tip the scales in favor of rising to see another day.

Each morning, I awaken with the expectation of something good happening. Does this mean I'm never hit with bad news or disappointments? No, not at all. They come with the territory and are handled accordingly. What I'm describing is an anticipatory attitude. My approach is to seek the best in every situation. I try my hardest to turn the gray skies blue. Most of the time I'm successful and on those occasions when I'm not, I acknowledge my shortcomings and move on.

I suppose this chapter can be summed up by saying it isn't what you see, but how you look at it that matters most.

From where I'm sitting, every little thing is going to be all right.

Chapter Twenty-One
The Road Ahead

THERE ARE DAYS when I lose myself in thought. Reflecting on my life up to this point leaves me somewhat bewildered. How is this quiet, shy, reserved girl now a published author? What gave her the courage to share her deepest, darkest thoughts and desires with the world? When did she arrive at a place of complete confidence in her abilities and total disregard for what others might whisper behind her back? Why is she suddenly brave enough to speak in public? These remarkable feats are only accomplished by extraordinary people, aren't they?

I suppose the answer lies in what sets these individuals apart from others. The short explanation is they possess a deep-seated belief in themselves and their capabilities. Regardless of what lies between them and their goals, they forge ahead as though the path is clear. What some would call "obstacles" are viewed by these determined minds as opportunities to grow. Each conquest translates into a lesson learned; to be filed away for future reference. No matter what they encounter along the way, gratitude emanates from within. What appears on the surface as a setback is used as a stepping-stone to a major comeback.

This sounds like some sort of elite group, doesn't it? Surely, I must be describing a rare breed; members of a secret society or club. They've had specialized training or conditioning which prepares them for greatness. Their success has to be the result of a privileged upbringing or hidden advantage they have over the rest of us. Whatever it is, they are anything but average citizens.

Every last word of the previous paragraph is based on common misconceptions. I am living proof of the transformative power of having faith in oneself. At the risk of being redundant, I am a regular person. I wasn't born with a silver spoon in my mouth. I was raised by honest, hard-working people who taught me the world owes me exactly nothing. Everything I own has been earned, sometimes through blood, sweat, and tears. I've survived being hurt and have inflicted pain on others. In other words, I am the epitome of normality.

Facing the hard reality of Tyger's death was my defining moment. I stared at the fork in the road, analyzing the paths laid out before me. One was lined with heartache, self-pity, and depression. It was a vacuum of loneliness, designed to hold me tightly in its grasp as a victim. I understood if I chose to go that way, others would feed into my misery. No one would blame me for deciding on this course. Showers of sympathy would rain down, perpetuating this eternity of anguish. I'd be accompanied by an endless supply of sadness as I made my way through the shadows. In this setting, motion would be optional and stagnation, expected.

The other path glimmered with the enticement of infinite possibilities. Although dim, the light shone brightly enough to catch my eye. It held the promise of healing which came with a single requirement: trust. I'd have to maintain faith in conditions improving. My pace would be of no consequence; the rule was to simply keep moving. Rest periods were allowed, along with the occasional good cry. The only stipulation was a willingness to brush myself off and continue on. Selecting this route would appear an unlikely choice to some, and become a source of inspiration for others. The abundance of hope was impossible to ignore, so I opted to proceed in this direction.

My soul assures me I chose wisely.

When I encounter those lost in the darkness, my heart goes out to them. Their torment is something I know well, so a silent prayer of comfort is offered on their behalf. I concentrate on lifting them through a sharing of energy. My intent is not to join them in sorrow, but instead, to demonstrate the possibility of becoming whole again.

The death of the loved one often leaves us feeling disconnected. This has certainly been the case with me. In the reconstruction process, I was pieced together differently. The woman I am today is an enhanced version of the one who existed before Tyger passed. My will to live comes as a direct result of surviving what I thought would kill me – the night his heart stopped beating.

I refuse to squander my time here wallowing in "what might have been." That doesn't mean I never wish we'd had more years together. Nothing would please me more. I've come to terms with his status as a spiritual being. Along with that comes the realization that I'll spend the rest of my days missing our physical connection. Rather than feel sorry for myself, I cherish the moments of the past and embrace our ongoing communications. Maintaining this outlook keeps me centered and on track.

This is what I strive to convey in my writings and when I speak. The mystery behind my ability to go on is based on a conscious decision I made to do so.

What's in store for me in the future? Absolutely anything.

I find such beauty in that. There are no limits except the ones we put on ourselves. I have goals and aspirations which I fully expect to reach. As the Universe conspires to make these things happen, my only job is to enjoy the ride. There is no joy if every second is spent looking for the next great thing. I slow myself down enough to notice the occurrences that brighten each day.

Growing up in New England, I'm accustomed to frequent, sometimes drastic, weather changes. There was a day in February when it was unseasonably warm. I could hardly believe my eyes when I started my car and the display on the dashboard showed an outside temperature of sixty-three degrees. Of course, I could feel how nice it was, but seeing such a high number in the dead of winter was shocking. It was lunch break in the middle of the work week, so I rolled the windows down and inhaled the mild air.

There was no way I'd let this gift slip past without enjoying as much of it as I could.

The best part of the story is the forecast for the following day. Every local channel was busy warning viewers of the Nor'easter, set to hit us and deliver more than a foot of snow. There was no possibility of avoiding the news; it was the topic of discussion with practically everyone. It seemed to me I had two choices. I could immerse myself in the moment and absorb every ounce of this gorgeous weather or completely miss it by worrying about tomorrow's storm. An obvious no-brainer, I chose the former.

As predicted, the next morning we were slammed with about fourteen inches of the white stuff. I can't say I was happy to see it, but I gratefully recalled filling my lungs with deep, cleansing breaths, less than twenty-four hours prior. What a disappointment it would've been if I'd missed out on that.

I apply this philosophy in all I do.

The best is yet to come and is also happening along the way to receiving it. The unfolding process of our dreams overflows with sources of pleasure. The issue with some of us is we can't see the forest for the trees. We are bombarded with exquisite treasures, meant to delight and inspire. In order to receive them, we have to be tuned in. It's taken a while for me to wrap my head around this concept, but I've gotten much better at redirecting my focus to the now.

Sometimes it's as simple as paying close attention to my breathing. I direct my awareness to the process of inhalation. Most often, I find myself taking shallow breaths. I clear my mind before drawing air slowly through the nose until my chest expands to capacity. This is held for several seconds before exhaling through the mouth. The goal is to push out every drop, before repeating the process. You'd be surprised how relaxing and beneficial this exercise is.

The relationship between Tyger and me is an example of what can be missed by fixating on the shine of a polished gem. We run the risk of overlooking a rough cut diamond which holds far greater value. Images of the ideal man or woman, designed and created to our exact specifications limit our availability when someone great comes along.

My Prince Charming didn't charge in, colors flying, on a noble white steed. He pulled up in a '96 Cadillac Deville and quietly, unobtrusively, swept me completely off my feet. I never saw it coming, not even for a second. This wasn't anything I could have predicted and physically we were about as mismatched as they come. I refer back to his appearance, which was well above average by anyone's standards. Solidly built, standing six-foot-five, he looked like a force to be reckoned with. Pair that with my five foot, three-inch frame and you'll begin to visualize the contrast.

The difference in size was completely irrelevant because ours was a blending of energy. Our souls felt familiar and we fit together like perfectly engineered puzzle pieces. The heat created through our union melted away every inhibition and the rest of the world be damned. At last, we had found one another. Finally, we had reached the summit, the absolute pinnacle of the tallest mountain. Not a thought was given to anything as shallow as the vessels that housed our authentic selves. If anyone found fault with it, they'd obviously never reached this nirvana or state of utter bliss. It wasn't anything we concerned ourselves with. We were too busy living and loving to worry about what others were thinking.

A deep sense of freedom is the ultimate gift we exchanged with one another. Tyger left his physical body, but this token of love will never dissipate. In his new life, I imagine him spreading his wings, exploring the far reaches of the universe. I intend to do no less on this side of the veil. Hills, valleys, and occasional turbulence are sure to come. I'll be wide awake and engaged through it all.

Once upon a time, I was afraid to fly, but my fear of heights has been conquered. A star is rising and I'm cruising right alongside. My journey is not limited to the mere desire of reaching a destination; the excitement lies in each milestone achieved along the way. The route may involve some unexpected delays and a few detours, but one thing is certain: it promises to be an exhilarating ride.

The instrument panel is set on success, skies ahead are clear, and it's all systems go. With an endless flow of gratitude supplying the wind beneath my wings... I intend to soar.

Epilogue

OVER THE COURSE OF MY LIFE, technology has made some major advances. I clearly remember rotary phones, black and white TVs with antennas, record players, and eight-track tapes. My memories go back to a time before microwave ovens and VCRs. I can recall my excitement when cable television became available in our area and how thrilling it was having access to so many channels. Waiting until Saturday mornings for cartoons came to an end because they were available seven days a week.

If I were to tell my granddaughter about these things, she would think I was describing another planet. As primitive as some of it sounds, I often long for such simplicity. It was a time when people spoke to one another. Children played outside and rode bikes with friends. There was no such thing as cell phones, but everyone still managed to keep in touch. Neighbors were like extended family members and looked out for the property of others. We knew practically everyone's name and which kid lived where.

Fast forward to the present and it seems with so much attention focused on all we've gained, little thought is given to what's been lost. Smartphones are capable of doing everything short of preparing a meal, yet we appear more disconnected than ever. Interactions have been largely reduced to texting which is fast becoming the preferred method of communication. This is unfortunate since these messages are so easily misinterpreted. Regardless of what the sender is trying to say, there is no guarantee it will be received as intended. This often results in hurt feelings and strained relationships.

While I enjoy using social media to stay in contact with family and friends, it is plagued by its own unique problems. Personally, I'm not bothered by what others choose to post. If it doesn't interest me, I simply scroll past or there is always the option to delete or block those we find offensive. It puzzles me how some are unable or unwillingly to do the same; opting instead to suggest what should or should not be shared.

In some cases, the perceived anonymity emboldens certain individuals. They gain a false sense of security as faceless entities typing on a keyboard. Much of what is said would be phrased differently in person. Little thought, if any, is given to the damaging effects of their words or any repercussions to follow.

There is no denying the enhancements technology has brought to our lives. We have the world at our fingertips which is wonderful, in moderation. The downside of having so many demands for our attention is it becomes all too easy to lose sight of the beauty directly in front of us. Priorities are skewed toward the rush of possessing the next big gadget.

As society clambers to keep up with advances, the family model is changing. Electronics have assumed the role of a babysitter or a tool to appease the little ones. Human interactions are reduced to a minimum, even between people in close proximity. It's impossible to strike up a conversation with someone who is oblivious to your presence.

My hope is it isn't too late for us to fix this. I refuse to believe our ability to speak face-to-face, exchange smiles, and make eye contact are going the way of the dinosaur. We can begin by simply acknowledging one another. A polite word or two is a start, even the old stand-by topic of the weather will do. All it takes is a few seconds of awareness to begin breaking the habit of isolating ourselves. It's not too late to reverse the desensitization currently plaguing society.

I made a personal decision to stop watching television news. Being fed a steady diet of negativity and tribulation is too draining on my supply of positive energy. By reading the occasional newspaper article, I'm furnished with enough information so as not to be completely out of the loop. Occasionally, I stop myself half-way through because the subject evokes sadness and/or anger. Those feelings are a signal that my peace of mind is in jeopardy and I'm due for a shift in thinking.

It's important to be careful of what we expose ourselves to. Even the strongest spirits among us can become contaminated by a constant stream of discontent. There are some who enjoy debating the latest political topic or playing devil's advocate. I don't fall into that category. I'm far too busy marching to the beat of my own drum to be concerned with what the next band is playing.

Remaining true to myself is what matters. I believe living by our own convictions resonates with other souls. Whether or not they agree, there is a level of respect earned. Sharing my experiences and ongoing connection with Tyger is done without hesitation because I was called to do it. Writing and speaking about this has become my passion.

Regardless of age, status, or where you are in life, it is never too late to pursue a dream. I published my first book at the age of forty-eight, one month shy of my forty-ninth birthday; this second book at age fifty. In all the years leading up to this, I never once aspired to be an author. Now, I can't imagine my life without writing.

I've tapped into a previously undiscovered love affair with words. It's a dance of sorts, playing with sentence formation, turning a colorful phrase, creating the perfect chapter title. I'm not exempt from the occasional writer's block but I so enjoy emerging from it. A fresh line of thought is exhilarating and I can go on for hours once the flow is restored. Plenty of long days at my desk have followed late nights of writing. Sacrificing sleep for my craft is not something I regret. This is my passion.

Do yourself a favor and figure out what moves you. That great idea you've been pushing to the back of your mind for years? Dust it off and give it a try. Take a chance without worrying about failing. Challenge yourself to step out of the box, well beyond the familiarity of your usual environment. This is what we signed up for in this earth school.

Diane Santos

Are you ready to go from surviving to thriving?
The perfect time is now.
I'll be cheering for you.

Recipe for a Joyful Life

Ingredients:

- **STAY GRATEFUL** – Gratitude is the key that unlocks the door of abundance. Begin each day by reciting or writing down all you're thankful for. The rate of attracting more will automatically increase. We are surrounded by endless reasons to be grateful.
- **CHOOSE HAPPINESS** – Yes, it is a choice. This is an inside job and you can start right now. Regardless of external conditions, focus on feeling good internally. You have complete control of your reaction to any situation, so be happy. (Helpful hint: re-read ingredient above)
- **BELIEVE IN YOURSELF** – The first step in achieving anything is believing you can. Have faith in your abilities and disregard the naysayers. Whatever you dream of can be yours by deciding to get out of your own way and go for it.
- **DON'T SWEAT THE SMALL STUFF** – Refrain from letting minor annoyances take root in your mind. That guy who cut you off in traffic is long gone. What's the point in stewing over it all morning? His day won't be ruined by your thoughts, but yours will. It's an insignificant blip on the radar of life. Let it go.

- **DON'T SUPPRESS THE BIG STUFF** – I'll always remember what the Dentist said about Halloween candy when my boys were little. "Allow them one good candy feast, then get rid of the rest. Much less damage is done in one sitting than small amounts over a period of time." Same logic applies to negative emotion. In the human experience, even the best of us loses control on occasion. Don't bury it. Have a long, hard cry. Yell, scream, or punch a few pillows. Feel it, push out every ounce, and be done with it. The rare meltdown won't hurt, it's the chronic ones that cause problems.
- **AVOID PEOPLE PLEASING** – What others think of you is none of your business. No matter what you do, someone is sure to have an opinion. Guess what? Not a single bit of it has anything to do with you. It's all based on how they feel about themselves. Live life with the intention of impressing yourself. Continuously strive to be better than the person you were the day before.
- **ACKNOWLEDGE YOUR ACHIEVEMENTS** – Celebrate your successes. Allow yourself to feel good about reaching a milestone. There is nothing boastful about self-recognition. We express this to others so there should be no hesitation when we've done something well. Reach around and pat yourself on the back, you deserve it.
- **ENCOURAGE OTHERS** – A kind word goes a long way. We have no way of knowing what anyone else is going through. Show compassion and lend a helping hand when

you're in a position to do so. We rise by lifting others and it feels great.

- **SHARE YOUR GIFT** – Sharing my personal story is done with the intent of inspiring anyone in need of hope. Each of us has been endowed with a unique ability which can enhance another life. Shine your light bright enough for others to find their way.
- **SEEK THE LESSON** – There is no such thing as failure, only opportunities to grow and learn. Even the best laid plans occasionally fall short. Use those stumbling blocks to build a staircase and keep climbing. View every perceived setback as a stepping stone to a major comeback.

Instructions:

1. Fold these ten ingredients into your daily routine until optimum consistency is achieved
2. Season with generous amounts of enthusiasm and positive energy
3. Allow mixture to marinate in your thoughts until application becomes effortless
4. Dig in and help yourself to a life of joy!

*** Serves YOU and all of humanity ***

PHOTOS

Michael Tyrone Johnson

"Tyger"

July 30, 1957 – July 30, 2014

"Forever in my heart"

~~ Surprise for Nani ~~

Sophia made this heart in the sand during our beach day on the second anniversary of Tyger's passing

July 30, 2016

~~Heartfelt Message~~

Later that day, we discovered this heart etched in the sand with "I L Y" (I Love You) inside. A sure sign of Tyger's presence

~~ *The Charlie Brown Tree* ~~

The belonged to Tyger and was given to me by his niece.
Sophia decorated it with love

~~ Family Love ~~

Christmas Eve, 2016, with my sons and granddaughter
Mark (left) Aaron (right) and Sophia in the middle

~~ A Voice is Found ~~

Speaking at the public library
East Lyme, Connecticut, January 14, 2017

ABOUT THE AUTHOR

DIANE SANTOS is an author and inspirational speaker. An avid reader since childhood, she never once considered writing a book. Her motivation was found following the sudden passing of her soul mate.

Her first book, *Onward into The Light,* details her grief journey and communications she receives from the afterlife. Choosing to focus on gratitude for this ongoing connection, she was introduced to the Law of Attraction. Diane is now committed to applying its principles and living a positive life. Spiritually enlightened, she shares her experiences to offer hope to those who can relate and are seeking validation.

Diane has discussed her story before a group of medical professionals and management at Yale New Haven Hospital, in New Haven Connecticut, as an invited guest in an open forum. In addition to speaking at multiple venues in her community, she has been interviewed on Blog Talk Radio's *Bridge Between Two Worlds.* Her work is also featured on *JoyfulToday.com,* an informational website which spotlights uplifting news and topics.

A native of Norwich, Connecticut, Diane grew up as part of a large, close-knit family. A mother of two and grandmother of three, she works full time as a receptionist in a physician's office.

In addition to reading, writing and public speaking, Diane enjoys floral arranging, long walks, and spending time with loved ones. Diane can be found online:

Website: www.diane-santos.com

Facebook: www.facebook.com/OnwardintoTheLight/

Twitter: www.twitter.com/DianeS_Author

Amazon: www.amzn.com/Diane-Santos/e/B01EDDP3AQ

Made in the USA
Columbia, SC
26 August 2017